Exponential Culture
Believer Transformation,
Disciple Multiplication

Michael L. Wilson

Exponential Culture
Believer Transformation,
Disciple Multiplication

Michael L. Wilson
Asian Access
Church Multiplication Catalyst
mikeexponential@gmail.com

ENDORSEMENTS OF *EXPONENTIAL CULTURE:*
Believer Transformation, Disciple Multiplication

Michael Wilson's *Exponential Culture* takes us beyond the usual analyses of how to multiply obedient disciples; its penetrating insights force one to think! It shows clearly and thoroughly how to make disciples that multiply, with vivid, effective examples drawn from experiences and research in USA, Japan, and Malaysia...

Had I read *Releasing Prayer Ministry* 40 years ago, my ministry would have been more productive and less bumpy. Believers who desire a more purposeful prayer life and a structured, thorough line of procedure, will welcome the exercises and enjoy following the specific guidelines.

- Dr. George Patterson, mission strategist and mentor

Beginning with the contrast between "casual Christians" and true disciples, Michael Wilson presents a beautiful case for relational disciple making. He bypasses cultural Christianity for something far better resembling salt of the earth. The book incites a search for very natural and effective pathways into the lives of people around you. Often this requires only compassion for the pain of others.

What makes the book so effective are the numerous stories of real-life disciple makers. His concept of disciple makers as "God-cooperators" brings life to the process of reproducing ourselves in others. "Holy gossip" is another highly organic tool springing from real people multiplying the gospel in others. Everything is built around establishing relationships—the word, 'barbeque' appears several times.

This book is a great tool for group-study and will bear fruit for all who use it.

- Ralph Moore, Founder of Hope Chapels

Mike Wilson's Exponential Culture puts 2 Timothy 2:2 into action as it lays out the character and capacities required for an authentic movement to result.
- Dr. Tom Steffen, Professor Emeritus
Intercultural Studies, Biola University

Mike came to Sabah Theological Seminary and Asian Centre for Mission in 2013, he taught a course on "Disciple Multiplication and Church Growth." To me, Mike has a dynamic understanding of disciple making from the Scripture, and based on his personal observations and experience throughout the years serving in the mission field and churches. He sees "relational evangelism" as the key to disciple multiplication process. The research on exponential growth of a tiny agrarian village from 20 people to a town of 5120 citizens is a powerful story of relational evangelism.

As a pastor, teacher and missionary myself, I fully agree that though "relationship building is time consuming, the mutually transformational process that happens during relationship building time is the strongest building block in disciple multiplication." Mike's real life experience, lessons and stories provide practical insight for pastors who would see their church become a Christ-centered church that keeps the Mission of Christ central and competently cooperates with God in His agenda of transforming His people into "little Christs" in this generation.
- Rev. Dr. Chen Lip Siong, Asian Centre for Mission (ACM), Director; Sabah Theological Seminary (STS), Lecturer; Serving in Mission (SIM), China Mission Consultant

"Mike Wilson grabs hold of that essential theme--the multiplication of disciples--and never wavers from it. Through numerous stories and examples, he brings the principles he discusses to life. Mike is a true practitioner and it shows: he knows what he's talking about. Lots of practical wisdom in here. Beautifully written, this important new resource takes us around the world, where those of us in North America can learn a great deal."
- Dr. Bob Logan, author of *The Missional Journey*

Discipleship is at the heart of Christ's call for our lives yet many have noted the lack of transformation seen in the American church today.

Here, Rev. Dr. Michael Wilson, church multiplication specialist with Asian Access and one of our most effective evangelists in Japan (Japanese pastors call him an evangelism animal), shares stories and principles that help point the way forward. He emphasizes that our personal transformation, day in and day out, as we walk with Jesus is core to seeing people, communities, and nations changed for hope and healing. Filled with insightful reviews of scripture, this book will help you as you seek to become more like Jesus and to be salt and light in our world today.

- Rev. Joseph W. Handley, Jr.,
President Asian Access, PhD Candidate

DEDICATION

I'm thanking you, GOD, from a full heart,
I'm writing the book on your wonders.
I'm whistling, laughing, and jumping for joy;
I'm singing your song, Most High God.
Psalm 9:1-2 MSG (adapted)

This book is first of all dedicated to the Bride of Christ for whom the Bridegroom bled and died and gave his Spirit to purify and empower. There is hope and blessing for reading to the end and applying what I believe the Creator of All is saying to His Church.

God has taught me much about both disciple multiplication, and church systems that are both effective and ineffective during 25 years of developing new churches in partnership with existing churches in Japan, sometimes called "The Mt. Everest of Missions."

Currently my work consists of helping with mission development and conducting workshops for pastors in an increasing number of countries.

Finally, I want to dedicate this effort to Mary Jo--my loving wife, best friend, and perfect complement to my God-given roughshod catalytic style. Dear, I love the way you keep putting up with me and I love when we can travel the world together in service of the King!

ACKNOWLEDGMENTS

This volume is much better for the efforts of my friend Noel Becchetti
who edited the manuscript and gave invaluable feedback.
I am very grateful to several men I consider giants of the faith who took
the time to read it in its less than fully polished form and then
wrote thoughtful, enthusiastic endorsements of the content.
This content has been taught to me by the Good Shepherd and
Lord of the Harvest, my Lord Jesus Christ whom I serve and
to whom I am eternally grateful.

CONTENTS

FIGURES

PREFACE

For some time now, the Multiplier had been sensing that God was preparing him for something. He had worked at the NASA facility for more than ten years and found the time fulfilling as well as lucrative enough to pay for his part time career as a seminary student as well as buy a house.

Even more than the work, Multiplier had particularly enjoyed his friendships in the workplace. Some of his colleagues seemed drawn to him when they were going through tough times in their lives. Multiplier could sense that the Holy Spirit was wooing a couple of his friends.

Nancy would often catch him right as he was about to go on break. As he listened, the Holy Spirit would urge Nancy to share some pretty deep hurts. She felt understood because Multiplier would listen carefully and repeat some of what she said back to her from time to time—to confirm that he was hearing her correctly.

Sadly, Nancy never surrendered her life to Jesus during the time Multiplier worked at the facility, but he could tell Christ's love and mercy had made a deep impression. When the time came for Multiplier to leave the facility, he could entrust Nancy's salvation to the Lord with a heartfelt prayer—and peace of mind.

George was another colleague who seemed to gravitate to Multiplier. They hung out together during breaks and after work—including an occasional Saturday, pursuing their common interests in hang gliding and rock music.

As their friendship deepened, Multiplier began to earnestly beseech God for George's salvation. As his prayers would finish, Multiplier would sometimes just sit and wait for something to come to him. Sometimes he would receive special insight into how to pray for his friend.

After awhile, something interesting began to happen. Shortly before a break time, Multiplier would, in the quiet of his mind, hear something like, "When you see George, tell him this….." Break time would arrive—and here was George with a question. But before George could ask his question, Multiplier said to George, "Before you ask your question, there is something I should tell you." He began to tell George what the Lord had told him, and as he did George's eyes got bigger and bigger. When Multiplier was done talking, George told him, "That's really weird! You answered my question before I asked it!" This happened at least half a dozen times over the next couple of months.

On the way to his car one day after work, Multiplier ran into George and several of his buddies in the parking lot. As Multiplier came up to them, George told his friends, "Hey guys! Here's my friend who keeps telling me the answers to my questions before I ask them!" And Multiplier proceeded to share the gospel of Jesus Christ with George's friends right then and there.

In time, many of George's friends accepted Christ through his continuing witness, as did George's wife, parents, two siblings and the sibling's families. George's warm, accepting friendship with Multiplier broke down his defensiveness about being "preached to." Multiplier's care for George and concern for his specific situation overwhelmed George's defenses. Eventually, the Holy Spirit gave George a passion to not only believe, but also to share the Good News with others.

This phenomenon of ordinary working people naturally sharing Christ in the workplace is occurring all over the world. Anytime we are ready and willing "to give an account of the hope within us" God's grace helps us and we come to know him better.

INTRODUCTION

The center of Christianity began in Jerusalem, encompassed the Roman Empire, shifted to Europe, and then migrated to North America. In the last three decades, we have seen the center of Christianity shift from North America to South America and Africa. Some of the largest churches in Europe today were founded by church planters who came from Africa.

The focal point of Christianity is now shifting inexorably back to the Middle East, where it all began. Millions of Muslims are trusting Christ as their Savior through visions and other signs and wonders.[1] Many Chinese Christians have a passionate vision to take the gospel "back to Jerusalem." Conversely, the Church in North America struggles to be an influence in an increasingly post-Christian culture.

This book will identify some causes of the North American Church's widening malaise and offer some helpful—and biblical—solutions, tested both domestically and on the foreign mission field. My passion is to see the Church in North America flourish and influence not only America, but also the world, for Jesus Christ. To do this, the North American Church must focus on transforming disciples of Jesus Christ in cooperation with the Holy Spirit, equipping them to be attractive, uncompromising and uncompromised ambassadors of the Redeemer--at home and abroad.

Jesus said if we remain with Him, we would be very fruitful. I will show why disciple multiplication is God's primary plan for those who remain with Him and bear much fruit. I will also share principles of disciple multiplication that have proven effective in both North America and Asia.

Relational evangelism is the key to the process. While building relationships is time-consuming, the mutually- transformational process that happens during relational bonding time is the strongest single building block in disciple multiplication.

---

[1] Joel C. Rosenberg. *Inside the Revolution* (Carol Stream, IL: Tyndale House Publishers, Inc. 2009) Kindle edition locations: 7043, 7268, 7271, et al

It is my conviction that more comprehensive character development and transformational teaching of the Word—teaching that motivates as well as it informs—is vital to right the North American Church's boat and stop its slow but increasing descent toward oblivion. The goal is not a return to the mono-cultural Church of the last fifty years. Rather, what is needed is a Christ-centered Church that keeps the mission of Christ central and competently cooperates with God in his agenda of transforming his people into "little Christs." Revive your Church, Lord!

1
ANY NATION'S CULTURE
REQUIRES MULTIPLIED SALT

You are the salt of the earth. But if the salt loses its saltiness,
how can it be made salty again? It is no longer good for
anything, except to be thrown out and trampled by men.
(Matthew 5:13 NIV)

When the Wilson family first headed to Japan in 1994, America and the North American Church were still in "Christendom mode." The Bible Belt and the Moral Majority were still strong national influences; TV censors watched out for us from a Judeo-Christian perspective; pedophiles were thought to be bad and pastors were thought to be good. People generally thought there was such a thing as absolute truth, heaven, hell, and one God. Jesus was thought to be the sinless Son of God.[2] Even then, true believers in Christ were a minority—as the Bible puts it, a *remnant*.[3] These are believers who know the commands of Christ and are committed to following them—even if they do not feel gifted in any special way.

In 2009, our family returned from Japan to a very different environment. We swiftly realized that the culture had experienced cataclysmic change in the time we had resided overseas. The culture could now best be described as *Post Christian*.

Watching TV, we were often shocked by what we saw. The media often vilified or ridiculed pastors and church members, and what once would have

[2] BARNA GROUP. *Post-Christian America?* https://www.barna.org/barna-update/culture/608-hpca#.Uw10Y_RdW3A
[3] George Barna. *The Seven Faith Tribes*. (Carol Stream, IL:Tyndale Publishing, Inc. 2009) Kindle location: 261-263.

been considered dishonourable was not only accepted, but was even promoted in public schools, the mainstream media, and the judicial system.

In his important book *The Seven Faith Tribes* based on a six-year statistical study of faith in America, Barna coins the phrase *Casual Christians*. Casual Christians purport to believe in Christ, have prayed a prayer to "receive Jesus as their Savior," but statistically their marriages fail as often as pagans, they succumb to substance abuse as often as the general populace, and they give almost nothing in offering for the work of God. This segment of the population makes up two-thirds of those called "Christian" in America.[4]

In the present era, faith has been stripped of supernatural manifestations which, though biblical, are suspect as something that cannot be corroborated scientifically—and therefore cannot be trusted. This pitiful excuse for biblical faith has resulted in churches that have been likened in Neil Cole's landmark book *Organic Church* to a mortally ill bride confined to a hospital bed, and with green pallor punctured with more than one IV in her arm as she waits for her Bridegroom in her soiled dress. In 2014, American and Canadian churches find themselves increasingly without influence. 80% of these churches have plateaued or are in decline.[5]

Is there an answer for the growing impotency of the North American Church? I believe there is--a holistic discipleship movement. It is a fresh wind from God, transforming first individuals--and, over time, neighborhoods, communities, and even nations. Discipleship that results in disciples making disciples making disciples—generation after generation—has the potential to reverse the deterioration of North American society and bring us back to a path that pleases God and promises his blessings.

What we need are communities of faith where every member—and leader—is a disciple of Jesus. In these communities of faith, we seek God's help to be transformed into the likeness of Jesus. We are all in this together and we all need—desperately need—God's gracious help.

Christ will refine us like silver or fine salt as we daily surrender all and submit to his leadership in our lives. The process can be painful, but his

---

[4] ibid. Kindle location: 272

[5] *Great Commission Research Journal*, Summer 2012, pages 6-42.

presence is "un-lose-able" and thus, comforting no matter what we face. Look at Hebrews 11, where it is written about some who were being sawed in half and sang hymns right up to the end of their supernaturally-aided-ability. They were comforted in their unthinkable but temporary suffering. And they had an eternal reward waiting for them once they had crossed over into the Kingdom of our Loving God. Maranatha!

2

GOD'S NATURE DEMANDS RELATIONAL MULTIPLICATION

God is the Triune God: Father, Son, and Holy Spirit. He is One in essence but he has manifested himself to humankind in three different ways as three different persons.

Various analogies have been put forth to try to explain this difficult truth. An apple has skin, flesh, and seed, but it is one. Water is found as ice (solid), liquid water, and water vapor—three that are often found in close proximity, nevertheless distinct, but one.

Dr. Hugh Ross, founder of *Reasons to Believe* and a worldwide evangelist and scientific apologist, likens this phenomenon to a superior entity revealing himself to a human computer operator who can only understand the two-dimensional image on his or her computer screen. To reveal Himself, God in this case might press his face against the screen, or poke a finger at the screen, or flatten his hand against the screen. God is still One being in his essence which can be compared to our human DNA—a composite of two personalities—which makes each one of us uniquely one being. In this analogy of God's nature, God has revealed himself as three different impressions—in reality, personalities—to our imaginary inquisitive computer operator.[6] I have no desire to resurrect the ancient heresy of "modalism," but only seek here to give us an analogy to help our finite minds try to grasp the infinity that is the One and Only God.

Adam and Eve conversed with Creator God as He walked the garden in the cool of the day (Gen 3:8). Jesus traveled mainly by foot with his disciples for three years ministering in many locations. The Holy Spirit comes to live inside us (John 14:3). He enters each believer and gives each of us gifts (1 Cor 12:13). Because of his three-in-one nature, God has always been in relationship.

---

[6] Hugh Ross, PhD, *Beyond the Cosmos*. Second Expanded Edition. NavPress. pp. 93-115.

He chose to make human creatures in his image—in relationship and for relationship.

The power of relationship has been grossly underestimated in our understanding of evangelism. Just as spending time enjoying God's acceptance and affection is transformational, similarly spending time enjoying the acceptance and affection of a friend changes us inwardly and prepares us to receive more. Research has shown that when a trust relationship is built in the process of evangelism, in most cases the "spirit of evangelism" is passed from the witness to the unbeliever much like a cold virus.[7]

In disciple multiplication, some are called to scatter their gospel testimony seed relationally, others are called to nurture the gospel seed in people relationally, and still others are called to harvest souls relationally—all the while in intimate partnership with the Spirit of the Lord of the Harvest.

In time one can grow in sensitivity to the Spirit's leading—the Holy Spirit who is convicting unbelievers of sin, and righteousness, and judgment (John 16:8) can help us "read" the ones the Spirit is wooing to Jesus.

---

[7] Michael L. Wilson. *Japanese Christian Multiplication, A Phenomenological Study.*

3
SCRIPTURE MANDATES MULTIPLICATION

> Listen! A farmer went out to sow his seed. As he was scattering
> the seed, some fell along the path, and the birds came and ate it
> up. Some fell on rocky places, where it did not have much soil.
> It sprang up quickly, because the soil was shallow. But when
> the sun came up, the plants were scorched, and they withered
> because they had no root. Other seed fell among thorns, which
> grew up and choked the plants. Still other seed fell on good soil,
> where it produced a crop—*a hundred, sixty, or thirty times* what
> was sown. Then Jesus said, "He who has ears, let him hear."
> (Mk. 4:3-8 NIV; Mt. 13:3ff; Lk. 8:5ff emphasis added)

The meaning of this parable is clear: "good soil multiplies." The other soils give us hints as to the different types of resistance or even hindrances we will face as we attempt to live as obedient disciples of Jesus Christ.

In addition to the Parable of the Sower (Matt13: 3ff; Mark 4:3ff; Luke 8:5ff), and Great Commission texts (Jonah 4:11, Matt 28:18-20, Mark 16:15-18, Luke 24:46-49, John 20:21-23, Acts 1:8), there are two additional parables of the Kingdom that strongly infer disciple multiplication.

In the Parable of the Mustard Seed (Matt 13:31-32 NIV), Jesus says,

> "The kingdom of heaven is like a mustard seed…Though it is
> the smallest of all your seeds, yet when it grows, it is the largest
> of garden plants and becomes a tree…"
> (Matt 13:31-32 NIV)

Commentators generally affirm that this parable talks about the Kingdom of God that starts out by taking root in an individual's heart, then expands rapidly so that nations can find refuge in the resulting transforming culture of peace.

This parable of dynamic growth in a relatively short amount of time seems to imply disciple multiplication.

Additionally in the Parable of the Yeast Jesus says,

> The kingdom of heaven is like yeast that a woman took and mixed into a large amount of flour until it worked all through the dough.
> (Matt13:33 NIV)

This parable tells us that the Kingdom of God— characterized by the transforming reign of Christ—permeates every aspect of culture: personal, societal, local, national, and even international. The yeast is small, yet mixes throughout the large amount of dough in a short amount of time. Such comprehensive dissemination and thoroughgoing transformation could only happen through the multiplication of change agents.

Returning to the Parable of the Sower (Matt 13:3ff; Mark 4:3ff; Luke 8:5ff NIV), Jesus says,

> "Others, like seed sown on good soil, hear the word, accept it, and produce a crop—thirty, sixty, or even a hundred times what was sown"
> (Matthew 13:8 NIV).

This is explicit affirmation of disciple multiplication by the Lord Jesus. It has been said that "Bad people make good soil." I believe even "good people" who are being transformed by the grace of God can become "good soil" disciple multipliers.

There is no other way to infect so many self-centered sinners with the transforming seed of Christ than a process that transforms the messengers even as they bring the message. This calls for holistic ministry that ministers to the whole person and discipleship that results in comprehensive personal and societal transformation.

Are you satisfied with the personal transformation you have experienced in your own life? The *Reveal* study done by the Willow Creek Association would suggest that the majority of American Christians—if they answered honestly—are not satisfied, and are left wondering, "is this all there is?" The results of this massive study of the North American Church go on to say that most American Christians plateau spiritually and either settle for transformation-less Church-based faith or leave the Church altogether.

I've met many former church members who don't attend church anywhere and it seems like they are not even sure if Christ is real. The good news is that it doesn't have to be like this. A transformational life in Christ can be ours—when we consecrate ourselves to seeking God for personal transformation and he makes us into disciple multipliers (Mark 1:17).

4

ESCAPING THE *ONE TALENT SERVANT* TRAP

The three Kingdom of Heaven parables in Matthew 25 give us a multi-faceted picture of how to be ready for Christ's return to Earth in power and glory. We find the first in Matthew 25:1-13:

> "Then the kingdom of heaven will be like ten virgins who took their lamps and went to meet the bridegroom.
> Five of them were foolish, and five were wise. For when the foolish took their lamps, they took no oil with them, but the wise took flasks of oil with their lamps. As the bridegroom was delayed, they all became drowsy and slept. But at midnight there was a cry, 'Here is the bridegroom! Come out to meet him.' Then all those virgins rose and trimmed their lamps. And the foolish said to the wise, 'Give us some of your oil, for our lamps are going out.' But the wise answered, saying, 'Since there will not be enough for us and for you, go rather to the dealers and buy for yourselves.' And while they were going to buy, the bridegroom came, and those who were ready went in with him to the marriage feast, and the door was shut. Afterward the other virgins came also, saying, 'Lord, lord, open to us.' But he answered, 'Truly, I say to you, I do not know you.' Watch therefore, for you know neither the day nor the hour"
>
> (Matt 25:1-13 ESV).

In this parable, God warns us to be, and stay, prepared--through the oil of the Holy Spirit's reign in our lives—in anticipation of Christ's return in glory. To understand what readiness means, requires a look at Christ's last words before he ascended into heaven after his resurrection. These are commonly called the

"Great Commission" texts (Jonah 4:11, Matt 28:18-20, Mark 16:15-18, Luke 24:46-49, John 20:21-23, Acts 1:8).

The thrust of these passages is that Holy Spirit-empowered believers are to be concerned enough to make obedient disciples as they go about their lives. There is no mention of special giftedness or even of a choice. The Scriptures make it clear that we are not our own—we have been bought by the precious blood of Christ (1 Peter 1:17-19). Many who experience the Christian life as boring would be convinced otherwise if they understood the mandate (and accompanying privilege) to be disciple multipliers in moment by moment partnership with Almighty God.

What follows next in the sequence of parables in Matthew 25 is a parable about the role of personal giftedness in the fruitful investment of our lives:

> "For it will be like a man going on a journey, who called his servants and entrusted to them his property. To one he gave *five talents*, to another *two*, to another *one*, to each *according to his ability*. Then he went away.
> He who had received the five talents went at once and traded with them, and he made five talents more.
> So also he who had the two talents made two talents more. But he who had received the one talent went and dug in the ground and hid his master's money.
> Now after a long time the master of those servants came and settled accounts with them.
> And he who had received the five talents came forward, bringing five talents more, saying, 'Master, you delivered to me five talents; here I have made five talents more.'
> His master said to him, *'Well done, good and faithful servant. You have been faithful over a little; I will set you over much. Enter into the joy of your master.'*
> And he also who had the two talents came forward, saying, 'Master, you delivered to me two talents; here I have made two talents more.'

His master said to him, *'Well done, good and faithful
servant. You have been faithful over a little; I will set
you over much. Enter into the joy of your master.'*
He also who had received the one talent came forward,
saying, 'Master, I knew you to be a hard man, reaping where
you did not sow, and gathering where you scattered no seed,
so I was *afraid*, and I went and hid your talent in the ground.
Here you have what is yours.' But his master answered him,
'You *wicked* and *slothful* servant! You knew that I reap where I
have not sowed and gather where I scattered no seed?
Then *you ought to have invested my money with the bankers*, and
at my coming I should have received what was my own with
interest. So take the talent from him and give it to him who has
the ten talents.
For to everyone who has will more be given, and he will have
an abundance. But from the one who has not, even what he has
will be taken away.
And *cast the worthless servant into the outer darkness*. In that
place there will be weeping and gnashing of teeth'
                    (Matt 25:14-30 ESV emphasis added).

It is clear from the context that the Master allots giftedness variously as
he wills to his servants—and no one is left out in the allotment. However,
it is equally obvious, that the Master expects— even demands—that each
servant do the best he or she can with the ability given them to *bring a
return on the Master's investment in them*. It is clear that gifts and results
vary, but God calls each of us to partner with him, and is not pleased with
spectators.

Let me emphasize: this parable is *not* saying that every Christian must
become a great evangelist. We are clearly not all gifted that way. Nevertheless,
our Redeemer King wants us to be involved in some capacity and earn a return
on his priceless investment in each one of us. Based on the Scriptures, it's clear
that God has a plan to empower and use each of us to play a role in extending

His kingdom through disciple multiplication. Notice that in the parable of the talents, the two servants who are affirmed by the Master *double their Lord's investment* in them—even though they are initially gifted disproportionately by their Maker.

The final parable in the Matthew 25 series—Parable of the Sheep and the Goats (Matt 25:31-46)—should alert every believer that there is no room for complacency in our life with Christ. The parable alerts us to the need to "walk the talk"—living as well as proclaiming the Good News of our Lord Jesus Christ.

In this parable, the Lord would have us be ready for his return by being a neighbor to everyone we encounter according to their need—even the least of these—through loving obedience to our compassionate King. This speaks to the importance of transformational discipleship—letting the Spirit change us from self-absorbed hedonists to the hands and feet of Jesus, willing to give up our comfort and even our very lives for others. A daunting challenge, indeed! Perhaps. But by responding to the loving prompt and assistance from God's Spirit, it is an awesome opportunity.

> "When the Son of Man comes in his glory, and all the angels with him, then he will sit on his glorious throne.
> Before him will be gathered all the nations, and he will separate people one from another as a shepherd separates the sheep from the goats.
> And he will place the sheep on his right, but the goats on the left.
> Then the King will say to those on his right, 'Come, you who are blessed by my Father, inherit the kingdom prepared for you from the foundation of the world.
> For I was hungry and you gave me food, I was thirsty and you gave me drink, I was a stranger and you welcomed me,
> I was naked and you clothed me, I was sick and you visited me, I was in prison and you came to me.'

Then the righteous will answer him, saying, 'Lord, when did we
see you hungry and feed you, or thirsty and give you drink?
And when did we see you a stranger and welcome you, or
naked and clothe you?
And when did we see you sick or in prison and visit you?'
And the King will answer them, *'Truly, I say to you, as you did it
to one of the least of these my brothers, you did it to me.'*
"Then he will say to those on his left, 'Depart from me, you
cursed, into the eternal fire prepared for the devil and his
angels.
For I was hungry and you gave me no food, I was thirsty and
you gave me no drink,
I was a stranger and you did not welcome me, naked and you
did not clothe me, sick and in prison and you did not visit me.'
Then they also will answer, saying, 'Lord, when did we see you
hungry or thirsty or a stranger or naked or sick or in prison,
and did not minister to you?'
Then he will answer them, saying, *'Truly, I say to you, as you did
not do it to one of the least of these, you did not do it to me.'*
And these will go away into eternal punishment, but the
righteous into eternal life."
(Matthew 25:31-46 ESV, emphasis added)

This parable makes it clear that God is not fooled when we praise him with
our lips and otherwise live totally for material success. There are many ways to get
involved in compassionate ministry to the poor, sick, imprisoned, etc. Again, some
are called to go, some support with impassioned prayer, and others give offerings
to support the work. I am blessed to be part of a mission that is well funded. My
heart breaks for all the homeless folks I see when I exercise my body on my bicycle.

Many more hands are needed to help the increasing number of poor and
needy in this country and the world. There are more people homeless and on the
move under duress than ever before in world history.

5

DEFINITION OF A DISCIPLE

Spontaneous expansion of the Church *begins with the individual effort of the individual Christian to assist his fellow,* when common experience, common difficulties, common toil have first brought the two together.
It is this equality and community of experience which makes the one deliver his message in terms which the other can understand, and makes the hearer approach the subject with sympathy and confidence
(Roland Allen, *The Spontaneous Expansion of the Church,* 1962, p. 10, emphasis added).

A simple biblical definition of a *disciple* is a Jesus follower. However, this is more challenging than it might seem at first look because to become a follower of our Radical King comes at a price.

Then Jesus told his disciples, "If anyone would come after me, let him deny himself and take up his cross and follow me."
(Matthew 16:24 ESV)

For example, how many of us are willing and able in any circumstances to live by the credo reported twice in scripture about Jesus and his disciples?

And Jesus said to him, "Foxes have holes and birds of the air have nests, but the Son of Man has nowhere to lay his head"
(Matt 8:20; Luke 9:58 ESV).

Or how many of us could act with compassion toward our attackers when under extreme duress like the time Jesus was being unjustly arrested by the Jewish religious authorities with swords and clubs?

And one of them struck the servant of the high priest and cut
off his right ear. But Jesus answered and said, "Permit even
this." And he touched his ear and healed him
(Luke 22:50-51 ESV).

These passages and many others make it clear that we each need
transformation. Too many of us are spiritual weaklings who no longer have the
"saltiness" of spiritual maturity—the fruit of personal transformation.

Mark's Gospel is generally considered the earliest written gospel account. So
his defining passage on a Christ follower is foundational:

Passing alongside the Sea of Galilee, he saw Simon and Andrew
the brother of Simon casting a net into the sea, for they were
fishermen.
And Jesus said to them, "*Follow me*, and *I will make you*
become *fishers of men*." And immediately they left their nets
and followed him
(Mark 1:16-18 ESV emphasis added).

The actions by a disciple, upon a disciple by Jesus, and then by a disciple are
once more outlined here:

1. Follow Jesus

We are to go where Jesus leads and do what Jesus shows us to do. Because none
of us have the character of Jesus yet, following him involves daily repentance
and re-commitment. But as we pursue a lifestyle of humble obedience, we will
experience the joy and powerful help of the Lord in new ways.

Growing intimacy with God characterized by recurring spiritual
breakthroughs can be our frequent experience. In *Experiencing God* (2008),
Henry and Richard Blackaby and Claude King report instances all over the world
where Jesus followers receive mysterious help, including signs and wonders, in
their service for God. In this current age more people worldwide are believing in
Christ through *experiencing him* rather than initially being talked to about him.

2. Become more like Jesus

As we submit to Christ's leadership and sanctifying work in each of us, we will be *transformed increasingly into his likeness and equipped for cooperation with him by his Spirit* (2 Cor 3:18; 1 Cor 3:9). This can be a painful process. But God is faithful and he will keep this promise and many others to those who commit to follow Jesus in any situation: "for it is God who works in you, both to will and to work for his good pleasure" (Phil 2:13 ESV).

Many churches I have worked with in Japan do *Elijah House Ministry* (Sandford & Sandford, 1982), *Deliverance Camp* (MacNutt, 1995) or other inner healing, deliverance, or exorcism ministries. In their prayer tool *Restoring the Foundations*, Chester and Betsy Kylstra help Christians deal with the four obstacles we face in our quest to finish the race well with Christ:

1) **Generational curses** (Ex 20:5): The sins of our parents still affecting us and our offspring up to the third and fourth generations.

   I had a chance to talk with a local church planter recently. As the trust between us grew, he shared that he had been born out of wedlock, some of his kids had been born out of wedlock, and now his oldest daughter had just given birth to her first child—out of wedlock. This is an example of the recurring pattern of heartbreak that often comes from generational curses still in partial effect. This is an example of the *stain* of sin that can remain operational even in those who have been freed from the *penalty* of sin by faith in Christ.

2) **Ungodly beliefs** (John 8:31-36): This is the mixture of truth and lies every believer wrestles with internally as we "work out (our) salvation with fear and trembling" (Phil 2:12 ESV adapted).

   For example, many of us who sincerely follow Christ experience too much stress about finances in spite of God's promise to his followers to provide for our needs (Matt 6:33). We hold erroneous beliefs in our heart that compete with the Truth of God's Word that sometimes goes no further than our head.

3) **Wounds of the heart that lead to unforgiveness** (Matt. 18:32-35 NKJV): Who has never been betrayed or deeply wounded by someone? Have you ever wondered how you can forgive someone who hurt you grievously? It can be so difficult that only a supernatural touch—or recurring touches—from the Great Physician can make it possible. However, scripture makes it clear that we have no right to hold onto bitterness. In addition it has the potential to pollute a body of believers (Eph. 4:31-32; Heb. 12:15).

4) **Demonic oppression** (Greer; Kreider, 1999): This is what awaits anyone who cannot successfully come to forgive from the heart, along with those who hold onto unrighteous vows or illicit soul ties.[8] The latter create trouble for us when we engage in sexual activity outside the covenant of marriage. I believe this also includes habitual viewing of pornography.

We can either cooperate with Christ in our deliverance (John 15) and give him increasing influence in our life, or we can self-destructively cooperate with the enemy of our souls— and give the evil one increasing control in our lives as we bend ourselves to his will (Matt. 16:19; 18:18; 2 Cor. 10:3-5).

In his incredible book *Maximum Faith*, statistical researcher George Barna makes the following statement:

So we now have a nation of more than 100 million "born-again Christians"—based on those who have said some form of a "sinner's prayer" and invited Jesus to save them.

---

[8] Chester & Betsy Kylstra. *Biblical Healing and Deliverance.* p.12.

Don't you think a country with 100,000,000 people who are
sold out to Christ would be a country that reflects biblical
standards and lifestyles? Wouldn't you expect a culture that is
bonded to the heart of God to lead the rest of the world to the
foot of the cross, by example even more than through words
and religious events? The relative unimportance of God's gift
in the scope of their life is reflected by the fact that so few
"saved" Americans bother to share Christ with nonbelievers;
worship God every day in significant ways; work tirelessly at
changing their life to avoid sinful opportunities and impulses;
and redefine their self-image to see themselves as followers
of Christ first and foremost. My research shows that most
Americans who confess their sins to God and ask Christ to
be their Savior—i.e., "born-again Christians"—live *almost
indistinguishably from unrepentant sinners, and their lives bear
little, if any, fruit for the kingdom of God.*[9]

Just like the pilgrims of old, we need help from on high to be faithful Jesus
followers—daily grace that keeps us on the path that leads to life, living water,
and spiritual fruit! The early American pilgrims knew that God needs our
affections in order to influence us amidst the temptations of life. What has your
own affections right now?

3. "Catch" people for Jesus

Jesus followers who have submitted to Christ's development process have attractive
lives that woo those around them. When a disciple of Jesus joins Jesus in his work,
they can do so with *character* and *competence* to empathetically share their own story
of God's grace in their life, and then as the Spirit leads to apply the Word of God
to the point of maximum impact in a lost friend's life. A believer with this kind of
magnetism has gone through a discipleship process that prepares their head, heart,
and hands for fruitfulness. They are compelled above all else by the love of Christ to
be an agent of reconciliation between God and humans (2 Cor. 5:14-20).

---

[9] George Barna. *Maximum Faith: Live Like Jesus: Experience Genuine Transformation.* 2011. p. 29.

6
GOD'S PLAN FOR HIS PEOPLE

For the kingdom of God is not a matter of eating and drinking, but of *righteousness, peace* and *joy* in the Holy Spirit, because anyone who serves Christ in this way is pleasing to God and approved by men (Rom. 14:17-18 NIV, emphasis added).

It is for *freedom* that Christ has set us free. Stand firm, then, and do not let yourselves be burdened again by *a yoke of slavery* (Gal. 5:1 NIV, emphasis added).

Even *as he spoke*, many put their faith in him. To the Jews who had believed him, Jesus said, "*If you hold to my teaching, you are really my disciples. Then you will know the truth, and the truth will set you free*" (John 8:30-32 NIV, emphasis added).

(Christ came) to rescue us from the hand of our enemies, and to enable us to *serve him without fear in holiness and righteousness* before him all our days. (Luke 1:74-75 NIV, emphasis added).

"The Spirit of the Lord is on me, because he has anointed me to *preach good news to the poor. He has sent me to proclaim freedom for the prisoners and recovery of sight for the blind, to release the oppressed.* This never-ending Truth of our Savior's mission overcomes the lies we all believe. He is in the process of *renewing the minds* of his followers (Rom. 12:1-2 NIV, emphasis added) so that we do not conform to the pattern of this world's thinking any longer.

Christ sets us free of the *strongholds created by unforgiveness and other unclean habits* that hold us back in our lives and service for him (Matt. 6:14-15; Matt. 18:34-35; Gal. 5:1).

Finally, for those who have become oppressed by demons (Matt. 18:35): *Christ frees those who cry out for His deliverance* (2 Cor. 10:3-5).

The Puritans who helped start America talked and wrote a lot about sanctification. This is the process of growing in holiness as one follows Christ (John 14 and 15; Philippians 2:12; Heb. 12:14). This process is initiated at salvation. This is shown in the following figure—a graphic representation of human beings that I call "Three Part Humans."

Figure 1. Three Part Humans

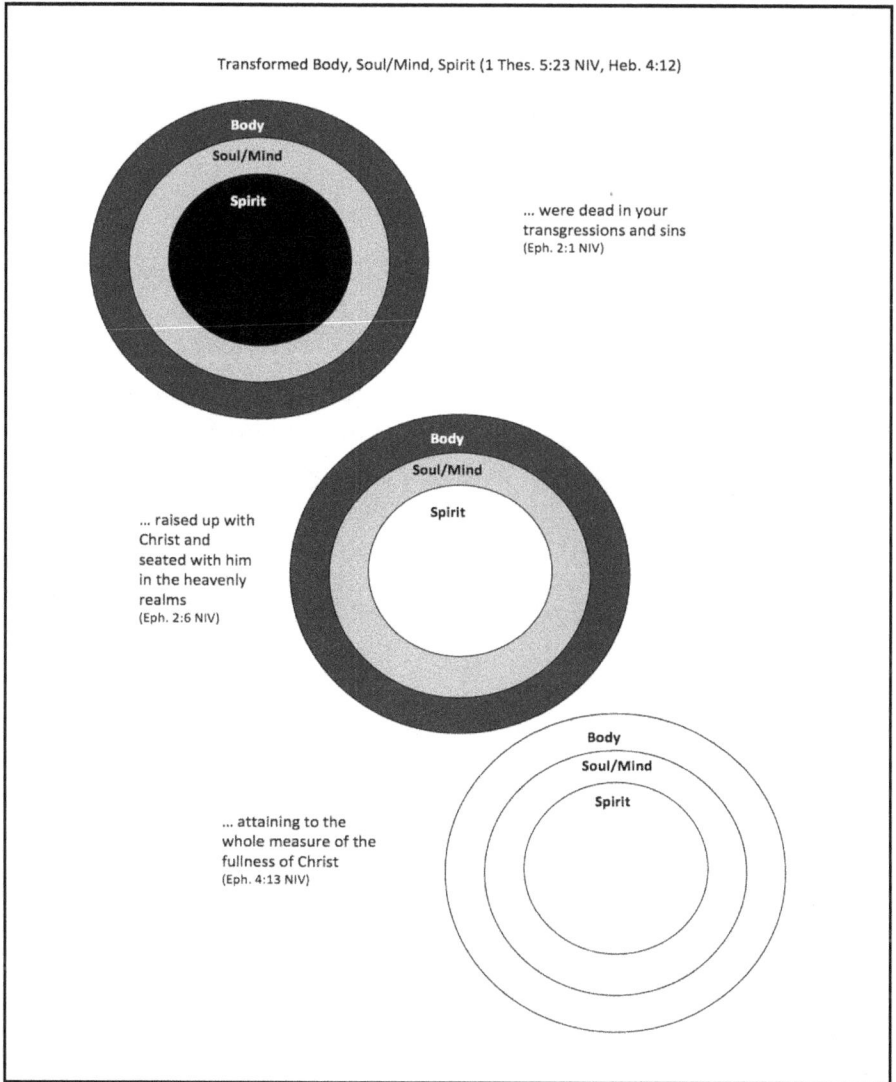

Transformed Body, Soul/Mind, Spirit (1 Thes. 5:23 NIV, Heb. 4:12)

Body
Soul/Mind
Spirit

... were dead in your transgressions and sins (Eph. 2:1 NIV)

Body
Soul/Mind
Spirit

... raised up with Christ and seated with him in the heavenly realms (Eph. 2:6 NIV)

Body
Soul/Mind
Spirit

... attaining to the whole measure of the fullness of Christ (Eph. 4:13 NIV)

10

---

10   Michael L. Wilson in *Great Commission Research Journal*, Vol. 2, No. 1, Summer 2010, p. 114.

25

Just as the scriptures clearly inform us, we are each one dead *spiritually* before Christ comes in and starts making us new from the inside out. We are new at conversion as Paul wrote in his second letter to the Corinthians.

> Therefore, if anyone is in Christ, he is a new creation. The old
> has passed away; behold, the new has come.
> (2 Cor. 5:17 ESV)

We now have a new capacity to sense God's presence and to converse with him in prayer. This new privilege is accompanied by a responsibility to tell others about this great new discovery. As time goes on in the life of a "God cooperator," he or she is "changed from glory to glory."[11] This is God's norm for his people—to be changed more and more into the likeness of his Son in whom he was well pleased until each one of us sees him face to face in glory.

---

[11] Michael L. Wilson in *Great Commission Research Journal*, Vol.2, No.1 Summer 2010, p. 118.

Figure 2. God's Plan for Humans: Glory to Glory

Transformed from Glory to Glory (2 Cor. 3:18 NKJV)

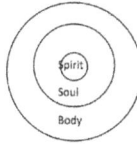

Spirit
Soul
Body

pure and without sin; clean and free from guilt; "not ashamed" Gen. 2:25 NKJV

Body, Soul/Mind, Spirit
1 Thes. 5:23 NIV
Heb. 4:12 NIV

As for you, you were dead in your transgressions and sins, in which you used to live when you followed the ways of this world and of the ruler of the kingdom of the air, the spirit who is now at work in those who are disobedient.
Eph. 2:1-2 NIV

to all who received him, to those who believed in his name, he gave the right to become children of God.
John 1:12 NIV

if anyone is in Christ, he is a new creation; the old has gone, the new has come!
2 Cor. 5:17 NIV

And we, who with unveiled faces all reflect the Lord's glory, are being transformed into his likeness with ever-increasing glory, which comes from the Lord, who is the Spirit.
2 Cor. 3:18 NIV

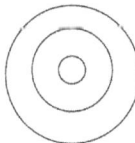

We will not all sleep, but we will all be changed—in a flash, in the twinkling of an eye, at the last trumpet. For the trumpet will sound, the dead will be raised imperishable, and we will be changed. For the perishable must clothe itself with the imperishable, and the mortal with immortality.
1 Cor. 15:51-53 NIV

The Scriptures in Figure 2 describe the increasing sanctification of the disciple abiding in Jesus Christ (John 14 and 15). When we as followers of Christ are being deeply transformed by the mighty power of God, and subsequently order our priorities aright, we can begin to tip the scales back toward righteousness in our environment.

A disciple is one who follows Jesus, is in a process of being transformed to be more like Jesus, and one through whom the Father and Jesus by his Spirit make obedient disciples (Matt. 28:18-20; John 6:44). In my experience, this process can be like riding a surfboard on a tsunami. There is no rush in the world that can compare to cooperating with God in his process of redeeming people one by one or in groups and then transforming them increasingly into his likeness.

There are many analogies for *disciple* in scripture: beloved son, beloved daughter, salt, light, sheep, saint, workman, servant, temple of the Holy Spirit, soldier, farmer, athlete, treasured possession, ambassador of reconciliation, and more. Nowhere is it written in scripture, "You are my beloved couch potato!"

There is a place for relaxation, recreation, and refreshment—just keep reading and see the model for holistic discipleship that God has given me for his Church! We Americans are world famous for our skill at relaxing, recreating, and feeding our senses.

The last words of our Lord's earthbound ministry, commonly known as the Great Commission does not say, "Make Christians." It also does not say, "Make believers." What our Lord's Great Commission to his Church does say is, "*As you're going throughout the world, witness* of Me to anyone you meet, and so make *disciples* of the ones who receive you (and me), *baptizing* them in the name of the Father, Son, and Holy Spirit, and *teaching them to obey all* that I have commanded you. I am with you to the end of the age and I will give you power for the work by my Spirit."

(my paraphrase of a synthesis of Matt. 10:11-13, 28:18-20; John 20:21; Acts 1:8, emphasis added).

It's just like worldwide church consultant Bill Hull writes in *The Complete Book of Discipleship*, "when the distinction between disciple and Christian disappears, so does the damaging belief in a two-tiered church. A disciple, then, is the normal Christian who follows Christ." To be obedient to Christ in the workplace, we will need to take risks. There may be a price to be paid sometimes.

As I write, Egyptian Christians are being tragically killed and their churches burned in that country. Reports have come in that in several such instances the surviving Christians—even in their grief—have painted on the remaining walls of their church, "We forgive you. We love you. Jesus loves you and he forgives you." As a result of this supernatural demonstration of the compelling love of Christ, tens of thousands of former Muslim perpetrators have repented and given their allegiance to this God of Love.

Sometimes the instrument of God's transformation in our lives can be a fiery trial of persecution or some other painful passage. In such cases, as we lean on the One who said he would never leave us, amazing ground can be won for our Savior.

As in 2 Cor. 4:1-2 NIV) Paul wrote,

> Therefore, since through God's mercy we have this ministry, we do not lose heart.
> Rather, we have renounced secret and shameful ways; we do not use deception, nor do we distort the word of God. On the contrary, by setting forth the truth plainly we commend ourselves to everyone's conscience in the sight of God.

Church programs can never transform members like this. It is close community—where every member and leader is committed to transparently growing (appropriately) in grace and intentional cooperation with our Wonderful Savior, by his Spirit, that can make us fit for supernatural redemptive service for him in any circumstance.

7

EXPONENTIAL: AN ALLEGORY OF DISCIPLE MULTIPLICATION

For many years, the population of the town of Exponential had been dwindling just as in many other rural towns. Young people chose to leave as soon as they had a driver's license and seldom looked back. But things had changed.

As I rolled into town, the oft-updated population sign caught my attention. I had been sent by a newspaper to report on the amazing phenomenon occurring in Exponential. In just 20 years, this tiny agrarian village that had withered to a population of 20 people had grown to a town of 5120 citizens! What had drawn the new folks? How might other rural towns grow again after years of decline?

It was my assignment to observe life in Exponential and interview the original 20 residents who had the best picture of the dramatic changes in town. The newspaper planned to disseminate the information obtained from the analysis of my interviews and participant-observation in Exponential nationwide in an effort to help other towns consider how to attain this kind of turnaround.

Figure 3. Exponential Population Sign

[12]

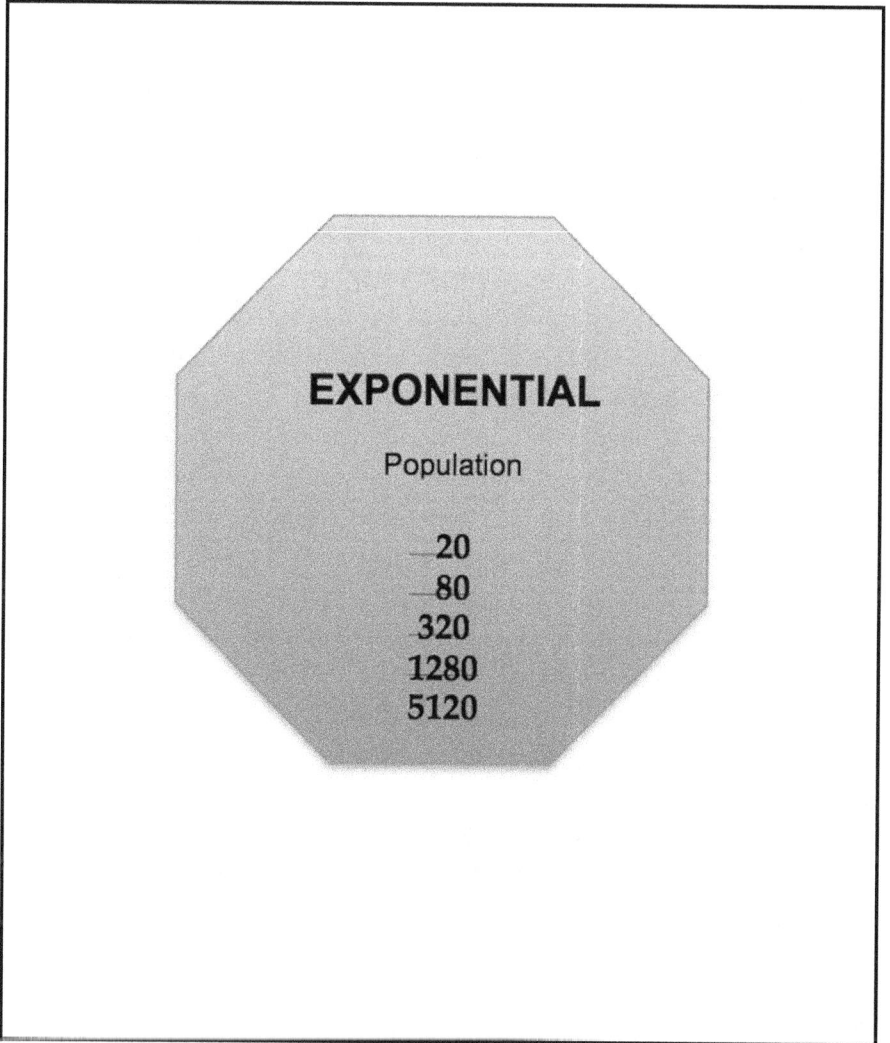

EXPONENTIAL

Population

20
80
320
1280
5120

---

[12] Michael L. Wilson, adapted from *Japanese Christian Multiplication: A Phenomenological Study, 2009*. Note: This is the actual rate of disciple multiplication by 20 multipiers who participated in the formal research.

To see more from ground level, I decided to walk the town looking for clues. As I walked around town day after day, I noticed that everyone I encountered was friendly. People would engage me in conversation, even when they seemed to be headed somewhere. They seemed genuinely interested in my situation and offered to help when appropriate. I saw genuine compassion expressed by townsfolk to a driver whose car had broken down. "What kind of place is this?" I thought in wonder.

Every one of the 20 original residents I contacted were eager to help me with my research. They wanted to listen to me as much as I wanted to listen to them. I was struck with the diversity of those whom I interviewed even while being impressed with their universal friendliness.

Gradually, the data I gathered coalesced around unmistakable themes. With this, an increasingly clear picture of how newer residents had come and how they in turn had brought in others appeared.

In most cases, a friend from town had approached an outsider while they were in the middle of a crisis of some kind--job, family, relationship, health, etc. Some newer residents reported a mysterious urging or experienced a series of coincidences that encouraged them to move to town. Several, after moving to town, immediately started inviting others—in a couple of cases the newcomer started inviting others even before they had registered their residency at city hall.

In some cases, the resident's story about the time before they lived in Exponential was hard to hear. Domestic violence, marital infidelity and abandonment, economic disaster, or terminal sickness had first opened up their thoughts to moving from where they had lived before.

These interviewees reported that their lives had dramatically changed after moving into town. One with terminal cancer had been healed as a resident prayed. Another had heard a mysterious voice urge, "Start your life over." Once she arrived in Exponential, she knew inside that this was the place for her to begin anew.

Some interviewees had been aimless young people with no direction and nothing in common other than a determination to not walk the same path as their workaholic, alcoholic, divorced parents.

Each had been approached by a town resident in a business or social setting and, through a process of being actively listened to, ended up coming to town for a visit. The vibrant hospitality and acceptance of residents captured these formerly directionless and sometimes rebellious young adults. Changed by the magic of the place, they themselves became vibrant, hospitable residents who welcomed other newcomers.

Around the time a resident invited them as part of their process of deciding to move, some outsiders had heard a voice from an unknown source; others were enveloped in a warm unseen embrace. Still others told me they felt they had found the accepting family they had always longed for but had never felt they had.

Eventually, a picture of how the original 20 citizens of Exponential multiplied became clear. In every case, there were three elements that led to personal adoption of the town:

> 1) First had been *a personal crisis of some sort*. This crisis created an openness to change.
>
> 2) Second, in the midst of their crisis, *a friendly messenger had come to each of them*. Most of the meetings were unplanned "divine appointments." Even though these meetings seemed to be by chance, the results were so powerful that most I interviewed felt there was some kind of destiny working in their meeting.
>
> 3) Finally, *wisdom was shared with them* by a town resident right at the point of need in their life.

Trust had already developed between the person in crisis and the resident who approached them. In every case, the person in crisis saw evidence of a desired benefit in the life of the resident that attracted them.

For their part, the residents felt they had discovered a joyful lifestyle that defied their earlier circumstances. The spirit of the place had changed them for the better—in ways too wonderful to keep to themselves.

There was nothing special or particularly gifted about these residents. They simply shared the benefits they themselves had experienced—just as we can do so as Christ followers who commit to be disciples who multiply disciples.

8

ROLE PLAY

> What then is Apollos? What is Paul? Servants through whom
> you believed, as the Lord assigned to each.
> I planted, Apollos watered, but *God gave the growth.*
> So neither he who plants nor he who waters is anything, but
> only God who gives the growth.
> *He who plants and he who waters are one,* and each will receive
> his wages according to his labor.
> For we are God's fellow workers.
> (1 Cor 3:5-9a ESV emphasis added).

When we arrived in Japan in 1994, my first jobs were to study the Japanese
language and pastor an international church. As part of my language-learning
plan, I would include in my daily devotional time a portion of time where I read
a passage of the Japanese Bible out loud. My faltering words were no problem
since, as most of us do, I conducted my time with the Lord by myself away from
others.

When I read 1 Corinthians 3:9 in my Japanese Bible, a light came on in my
mind. *Fellow worker* in the English Bible is rendered *cooperator* in Japanese. I
realized that my fundamental purpose in ministry is to **cooperate** with God in
His ministry. I need to be aware of what God is doing in those around me and
adjust my life to join in with his agenda in their lives.

Like you, I'm a flawed human. I resist God's working to reorder my
priorities and complain about seemingly senseless pain I suffer. However, I've
come to know God in a deeper, more intimate way as I've persisted in joining
him in his work of redemption.

Once I'm clear as to my purpose, I can begin to figure out my *role*—
the particular part I will play in God's Kingdom agenda. Our roles can be
determined through a number of factors.

The first factor is *giftedness.* No matter what kind of talents God gives us, it is clear from 1 Corinthians 12 and other passages that we each have a unique allotment of spiritual or *grace gifts* given us by the Holy Spirit. Whatever God has for us, there is fruit awaiting—both qualitative and quantitative—as we put our hands to the plow and cooperate with our awesome Master.

In 1994, we had a large group of new missionaries in Japan. Together we studied the *Network* assessment of spiritual gifts, spiritual passion, and spiritual style.[13]

What I discovered during those first few days in Japan still holds true: I exist to move people closer to God. If someone doesn't know Christ, I want to introduce them. If someone knows Christ, I want them to know him more and love him more. This divinely-appointed role has consistently motivated me through 25 years of church planting, multiplying disciples, and training church planters—and is the motivation behind me writing this book.

The second factor in determining our redemptive role is discerning our spiritual *style.* Our style tells us *how* we will do what God created us to do. This is best discovered while trying out different ministries and methods. What has resonated with you? How were you used most effectively? *Giftedness* and *style* together will determine what specific role you play in developing multipliers.

For example, do you have good communication skills? Are you generally outgoing? Are people drawn to you, or at least comfortable with you? In this case, you might be a *closer* or spiritual harvester in the final process of welcoming new multipliers into the worldwide family of God.

Maybe you're a *nurturer.* You draw people strongly by your hospitality or thoughtfulness. In that case, you might nurture people closer to Christ by your cooperation with the Holy Spirit. Nurturers often have a habit of saying just the right thing to put someone at ease or to make them think more deeply.

All believers are called to *scatter seed*—little testimonies of God's daily blessings in their life. How each of us do this (according to our giftedness and style) is what gets the team sport of disciple development rolling. It usually takes many touches by the gospel for someone to finally give up their resistance and embrace Christ.

[13] Bruce Bugbee. *Discover Your Spiritual Gifts the Network Way: 4 Assessments.* 2005.

Every salvation is a Holy Spirit miracle (John 3:3, 5; 6:44, 65). But God chooses to use each of us in a naturally-relational process to woo outsiders into the greatest fellowship in the universe! And when we allow God to use us to woo our family, friends, co-workers, and others to Christ, we experience God's grace in amazing new ways (Philemon 6 NIV).

God has given each church a unique mix of gifts, cultures, styles, passions, and even destinies. He will shape our specific collective and individual strategies of developing disciples who multiply as we cooperate with him. Such a Church culture will be characterized by relational networks that encourage and equip and deploy disciples naturally into the harvest.

A church with a culture of disciple multiplication will keep the main thing the main thing—loving our neighbors at their point of need and nurturing our own relationships with Jesus so we have blessings to share as we draw our neighbors to the Savior.

9

LISTENING TO GOD

A great asset for disciple multiplication is being able to hear God's voice. An untruth I have heard many times from believers is that "I could never hear God's voice. He just does not talk to me that way." I believe scripture teaches differently.

Notice the references to Jesus' "sheep" in John 10:1-4 ESV (emphasis added).

> "Truly, truly, I say to you, he who does not enter the sheepfold by the door but climbs in by another way, that man is a thief and a robber.
> But he who enters by the door is the shepherd of the *sheep*.
> To him the gatekeeper opens. *The sheep hear his voice, and he calls his own sheep by name and leads them out.*
> When he has brought out all his own, he goes before them, and *the sheep follow him, for they know his voice.*

John 10:1-28 makes four clear references to *sheep* hearing and recognizing the voice of the Good Shepherd Jesus (vss. 3,4,16,27), and two very clear converse statements about not hearing the Shepherd (vss. 5,8) and why this is so (vs. 26). If you carefully think about this, do you still want to say you cannot hear the voice of God—ever?

When we learn to listen to God, exciting adventures await—powerful pre-evangelistic encounters that can move spiritually-unconcerned people to consider for the first time that there might be a God who cares about them. That's often how the process toward disciple multiplication starts. (Check out a wild account of pre-evangelism in Appendix II: Spiritual Treasure Hunting).

How many people are out there who have never really heard that God loves them, but who could be blessed by a gentle but bold approach that powerfully communicates that truth to their waiting heart? This kind of approach is particularly effective in a pantheistic culture like Japan or post-Christian ones like the USA and Canada. The cultural distance between a Christian with a biblical worldview and a non-Christian with a radically different worldview can be bridged by gentle but bold attempts to show compassion in an atmosphere of acceptance.

More often than not, nonreligious people can become open to the idea of a God who values them and has reached out to them unexpectedly. I have noticed recently that several people I have been praying for for decades are more open to discussing spiritual things than ever before. God is softening the hard hearts of the human race at this time in history. Empathetic witnesses who use a relational approach can accomplish more than they previously could have thought or imagined.

10

HOLISTIC DISCIPLESHIP

And he gave the apostles, the prophets, the evangelists, the
pastors and teachers, *to equip the saints for the work of ministry*,
for building up the body of Christ, until we all attain to the unity
of the faith and of the knowledge of the Son of God, to mature
manhood, to the measure of *the stature of the fullness of Christ.*
(Ephesians 4:11-13 ESV, emphasis added).

There is neither Jew nor Greek, there is neither slave nor free, there
is neither male nor female, for you are all one in Christ Jesus.
(Galatians 3:28 ESV)

If Paul were writing a letter to the Church in North America today, he
might write something like, "There is neither black nor white, there is neither
Evangelical nor Pentecostal, there is neither laity nor clergy, there is neither male
nor female, for you are all one in Christ Jesus." God is bringing a new unity to
his Church in this age that transcends race, gender, and pet theologies.

In Tohoku, Japan, Conservative Baptists are cooperating with Pentecostals
and Presbyterians to develop new communities of faith to bring hope to the
devastated. In the USA, some churches are closing and others are declining, but
still others are working together to an unprecedented degree.

A growing number of churches enjoy diverse ethnic and generational faith
communities worshipping together on one church campus and, in some cases,
reaching out together to rapidly changing neighborhoods where many of the
newcomers do not speak English. God has brought "Samaria and beyond" to
our local neighborhoods and elements of the Church are working hard to reach
out compassionately and coherently within this new context.

Young people in thriving churches reject the "safe" religion of their elders in
favor of a faith where prophetic prayer and healing grace are often seen. Ministry

teams go out from churches like this worldwide to do battle with sex trafficking and substance abuse, and to make the beauty of Christ known to those who had never even considered him. They are learning to embrace a holistic theology that encompasses the whole Word of God for today—one that is appropriately *contextualized* to connect with a diverse and multicultural world.

Faith still comes by hearing the Word of God, but we need the Holy Spirit to help us know what portion of the Good News is the appropriate "bait" or "balm" for each person he is leading us to draw to Christ. The importance of context is also true of biblical interpretation. To communicate effectively, we must be aware of the culture, perspective, and worldview of those listening.

Paul did this when he wrote to Timothy telling him, "Be diligent to present yourself approved to God, a worker who does not need to be ashamed, rightly dividing the word of truth" (2 Timothy 2:15 NKJV). Timothy, a younger man who was half Jewish, had considerable exposure to the Hebrew Scriptures and was familiar with the Jewish worldview shaped by his forefathers' time in the wilderness with God leading the way with a pillar of cloud and pillar of fire. He had been taught by his godly grandmother and mother how the Israelites had crossed the Jordan River at flood stage miraculously on dry ground. So he had an expectation of spiritual power from God. What he needed were the safe boundaries provided by the Word of God already written in the Old Testament and being written at that time in the New Testament.

Conversely, Paul asserted to the Corinthian Greeks (who loved to debate ideas and were versed in diverse schools of thought cf. Acts 17:21; 1 Cor. 1:22), "For the kingdom of God is not a matter of talk but of power" (1 Cor. 4:20, also 2:4-5 NIV) and "imitate me" (1 Cor. 4:16 NIV). Paul calls the Corinthians not to more talk, but to godly living and hands-on ministry accompanied by expectations of God's mighty power. This type of thing is usually associated with Charismatic Christians or Pentecostals but really, it's just biblical.

Ephesians 4:13 makes clear that the role of pastor, teachers, prophets, and evangelists is to develop new believers to maturity in Christ equipping them for effective service. In that spirit, let me introduce a model for holistic discipleship that results in transformation--disciple multipliers who are seed scatterers, nurturers, and harvesters with both character and competence.

Figure 4. Holistic Discipleship

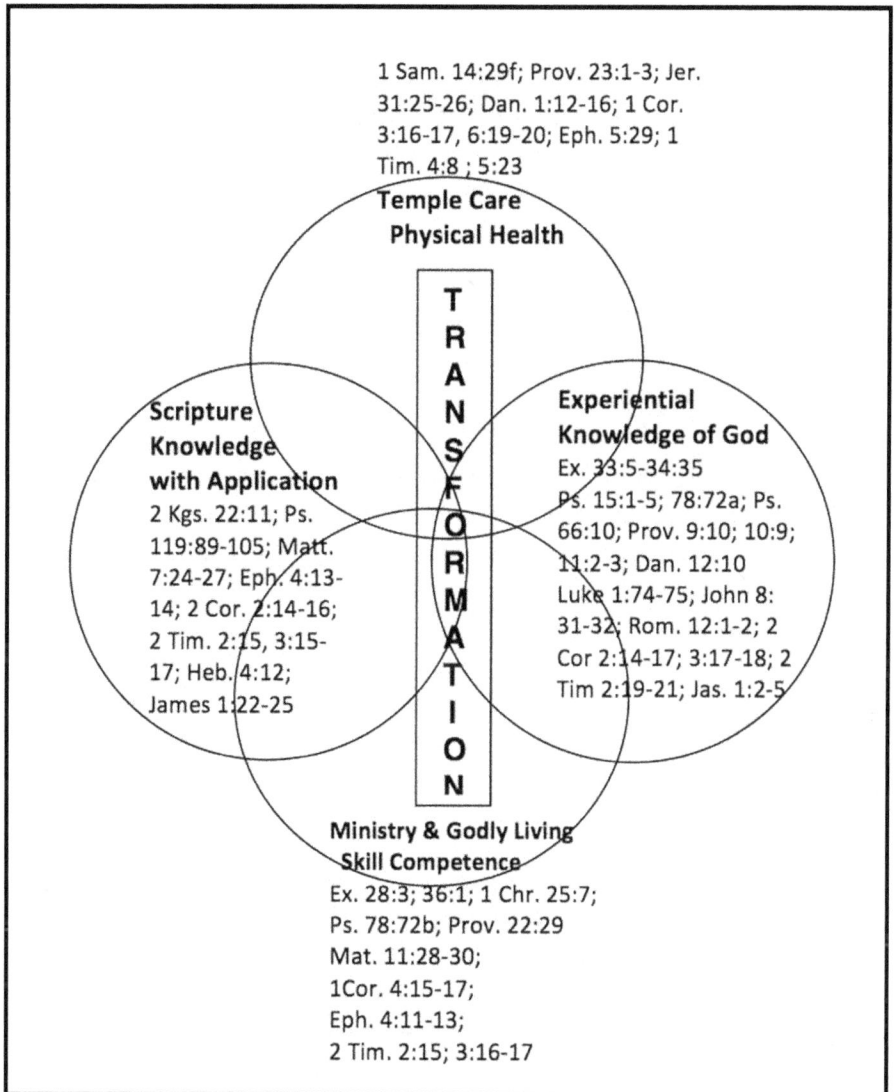

1 Sam. 14:29f; Prov. 23:1-3; Jer. 31:25-26; Dan. 1:12-16; 1 Cor. 3:16-17, 6:19-20; Eph. 5:29; 1 Tim. 4:8 ; 5:23

Temple Care
Physical Health

T R A N S F O R M A T I O N

Scripture Knowledge with Application
2 Kgs. 22:11; Ps. 119:89-105; Matt. 7:24-27; Eph. 4:13-14; 2 Cor. 2:14-16; 2 Tim. 2:15, 3:15-17; Heb. 4:12; James 1:22-25

Experiential Knowledge of God
Ex. 33:5-34:35 Ps. 15:1-5; 78:72a; Ps. 66:10; Prov. 9:10; 10:9; 11:2-3; Dan. 12:10 Luke 1:74-75; John 8: 31-32; Rom. 12:1-2; 2 Cor 2:14-17; 3:17-18; 2 Tim 2:19-21; Jas. 1:2-5

Ministry & Godly Living Skill Competence
Ex. 28:3; 36:1; 1 Chr. 25:7; Ps. 78:72b; Prov. 22:29 Mat. 11:28-30; 1Cor. 4:15-17; Eph. 4:11-13; 2 Tim. 2:15; 3:16-17

When we grow in all four areas mandated by God's Word, we are like a multi-faceted gem. We are like an attractive book people want to read that points the way to the Son of God, the Christian's Savior and King.

As shown Figure 4 consists of four circles representing the areas of growth mandated for God's people: *Temple Care, Experiential Knowledge of God, Ministry & Godly Living Skill Competence,* and *Scripture Knowledge with Application.* The four circles intersect—they interact with one another. Their combined effect leads to synergistic growth and personal transformation. When we are deficient in one area, it negatively affects the others. There is a synergy that comes from strengthening and exercising one or more of the areas in cooperation with Holy Spirit.

This type of discipleship is especially needed in churches under the threat of persecution to develop disciples who will be faithful and even fruitful in any circumstance. Leadership of the Church in such countries must be decentralized. What that means is believers must grow in head, heart and hands to the point where relational networks can be developed that function under submission to the leadership but independently in everyday functions. In such a church, even if the "head" is cut off by persecution, the church will not die but continue to thrive by the grace of God as each part of the body does it's part. Someone has said, "Looking at fulfilling the Great Commission: The first third was easy, the second third is hard, the last third will be bloody." We are definitely in the last third now and there's no telling when the Western Church will be called on to join the Church in the majority of countries that grow "by the blood of the martyrs."

The important question right now is how can a model like this work in real life? To develop a balanced approach to discipleship, church systems must be considered. Once we identify a need or problem in the process of making disciples who make disciples, strategy, process, and mechanism must be developed and employed that will achieve the desired outcomes.

For that reason, at the end of the discussion of each of the four areas of mandated growth, I've offered some proven guidelines, principles, and methodologies for developing disciples in each area in any church culture: affluent, impoverished, persecuted or politically favored.

Temple Care: Physical Health

When we lived in Japan, we did not own a car for seven of the seventeen years. During that time, I rediscovered my youthful love affair with the bicycle. While it was sometimes a challenge to juggle bicycle, backpack with Bible study materials, and self—especially in the snow—my health and energy level were as good as they had ever been.

Upon our return to the USA after our seven-year church planting assignment in Tokyo, I took a mandatory physical exam early in our time at home. I was then 50 years old and wondered what kind of shape I was in. After the tests, the doctor came into the room. The first thing he said to me was, "Tell me your secret." My blood cholesterol was good—for a 20 year old! Some of this is genetic, but my years riding a bicycle as my main mode of transportation had resulted in a glowing physical report.

When we neglect our bodies, we pay a price. We cannot concentrate. Our weight can get out of control. We get winded just walking across the parking lot to the car. When I don't get enough sleep, it can really affect not only my performance, but also my peace of mind.

We could have accountability partners for mutual encouragement in developing self-discipline in terms of physical health. There are some really helpful smartphone apps. I really like *My Fitness Pal.* As I make taking care of my body a priority, I find I have a lot more energy and joy to serve God.

God's Word has a lot to say about care of our physical being. After all, it's the part of us that God made to interact with his physical creation. It is the Temple of the Holy Spirit.

Figure 5. Temple Care: Physical Health

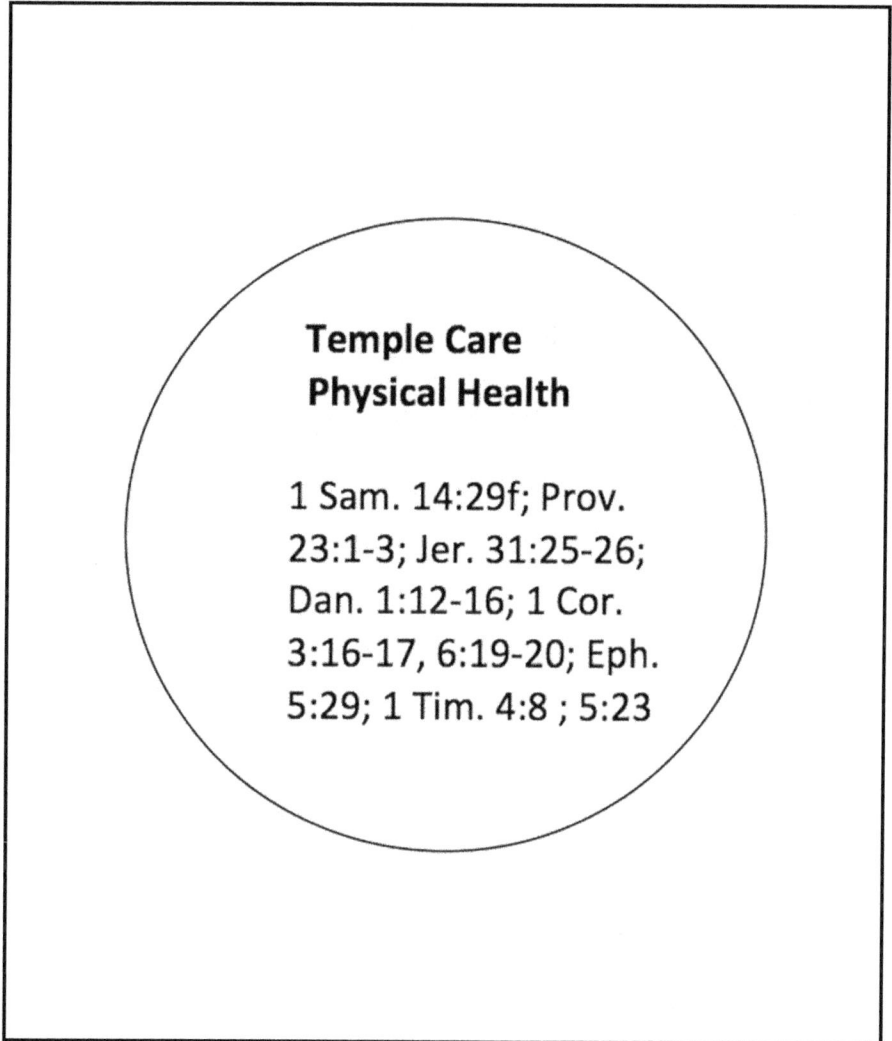

**Temple Care
Physical Health**

1 Sam. 14:29f; Prov. 23:1-3; Jer. 31:25-26; Dan. 1:12-16; 1 Cor. 3:16-17, 6:19-20; Eph. 5:29; 1 Tim. 4:8 ; 5:23

We are three-part beings made in God's image: body, spirit, and soul/mind/ heart (1 Thessalonians 5:23; Hebrews 4:16). All three must be cared for and developed for each of us to function the way God intends.

It is truly amazing the benefits we can derive from regular moderate physical exercise and a reasonable diet. In the Church, we can mentor one another about taking care of our health, and how to do it. Why not build fitness classes into church life, using the gifts of physical trainers in our congregations? Customized exercise programs could be designed that take into account work, family, and other obligations. Certainly, such a commitment would leave a lot less time for sitting in front of the TV.

A commitment to personal health and fitness can also provide wonderful outreach opportunities. When I'm on my bike, I sometimes have "divine appointments" with people the Holy Spirit has led to cross paths with me. As we get out and play redemptively in the world, God will put us in situations where disciple multiplication can naturally happen—and our bodies will be the better for it!

Experiential Knowledge of God

A major challenge for many North American Christians is accepting and embracing the experiential aspects of our faith. The Modernist deification of the human mind can make the concept of spiritual power seem superstitious. Hence, the Apostle Paul's exhortation to the intellectually-oriented Corinthian Greeks is of special importance to us:

> My message and my preaching were not with wise and persuasive words, but with a demonstration of the Spirit's power, so that your faith might not rest on men's wisdom, but on God's power.
>
> (1 Corinthians 2:4-5 NIV)

> For the kingdom of God is not a matter of talk but of power.
>
> (1 Corinthians 4:20 NIV)

My research, conducted both in America and Japan, suggests that when someone believes Christ for the first time as a result of a demonstration of the Spirit's power, they are quite excited and sure of God's reality and love for them. This first hand testimony of God's power and love is a potent motivator to testify to others.

Conversely, when a Christian attempts to convince someone of the gospel on intellectual persuasion alone, they can often be suspected of "selling something." Those with an intellectual bent can sometimes be convinced by the second hand testimony, but for faith to stick, direct experience with the Spirit of God can be vital—so that their faith might not rest on men's wisdom, but on God's power.

In addition, Christ invites us to interact with him in prayer. As I have already stated, I believe John Chapter 10 makes it clear that anyone who knows Christ and has his indwelling Holy Spirit can hear and recognize God's voice when he talks to us. I have seen cancer patients become vibrant after prayer even though God had not healed their physical "God-sized horror." Both myself and others have seen impediments that kept us from fulfilling Christ's divine purpose removed with just an intimate word from Christ. Once after my mother had passed from aspects of dementia or Alzheimer's, I woke up in a cold sweat and Christ whispered a word to me that removed the fear of such mind loss forever.

Here I present a flowchart of interactive prayer developed by friends at Evergreen Baptist Church San Gabriel Valley that has been used for heart change in believers on several continents and to help non-Christians "taste and see the Lord is good."

Figure 6. Releasing Prayer Ministry

PRAYER THAT TRANSFORMS THE HEART (PSALM 46:10;
MATTHEW 16:19; JOHN 10:3, 4, 8, 14, 16, 27)

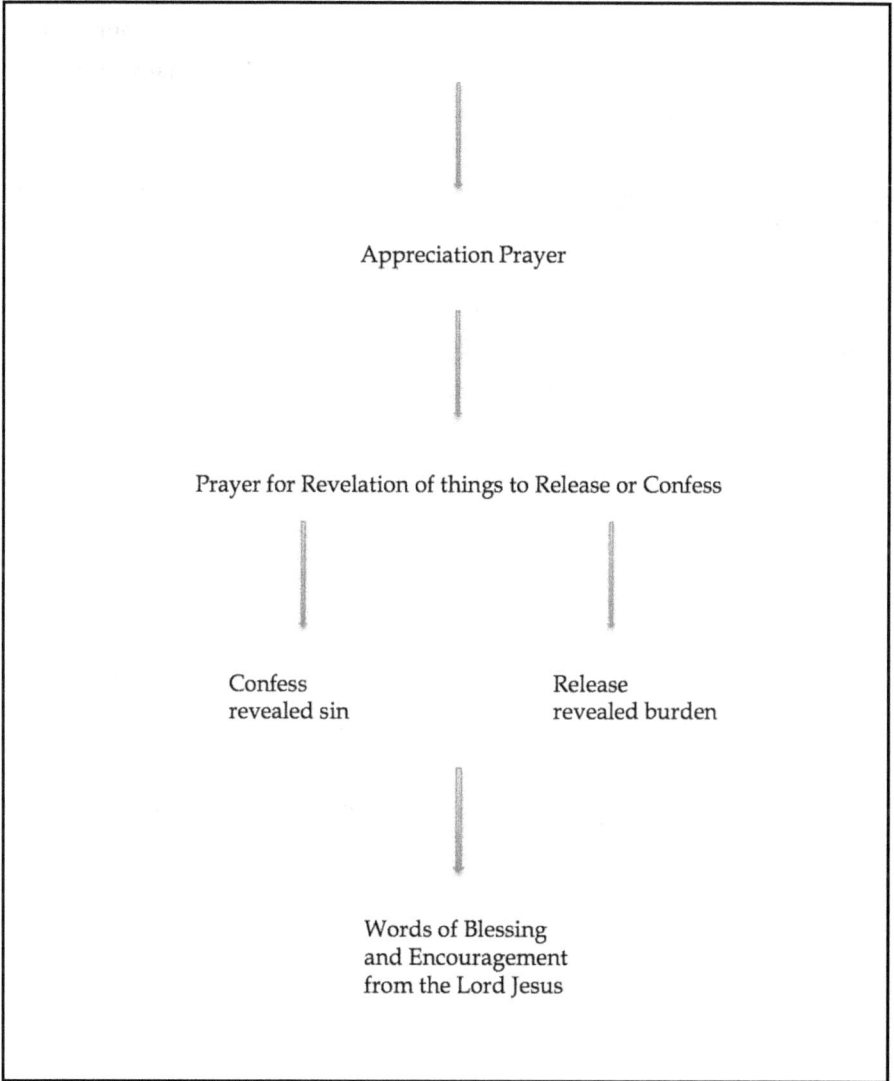

Appreciation Prayer

Prayer for Revelation of things to Release or Confess

Confess
revealed sin

Release
revealed burden

Words of Blessing
and Encouragement
from the Lord Jesus

In particular the last prayer in the flowchart can transform a person on the spot. In my experience in several countries, God loves to say words of blessing and encouragement to his dear children and when he does they can be changed forever—no matter what kind of dire situation they may be facing. Sometimes even a non-Christian who was chosen by God before the beginning of time (1 Cor. 2:7; Eph. 1:11; 1 Peter 1:1:1-2) can hear him affirming and encouraging them when we pray, "Lord, would you just tell my friend here what you think of her/him." It's always very encouraging even over the phone.

A great experiment is to attempt to live in moment-by-moment awareness of God. Frank C. Laubach did this while he was working in the Philippines. His diary tells of his struggles[14] to stay in intimate connection with Christ amidst the struggles of life in another culture. Frank's writings go on to tell about his later life where God just kept expanding his sphere of influence as he learned to not be rocked by circumstances, but to truly rest in the shadow of Christ's wings— no matter what—and let Christ's unimaginable power flow through him.

[14] Frank Charles Laubach. 1964. *Frank Laubach's Prayer Diary.*

Figure 7. Experiential Knowledge of God

Experiential Knowledge of God

Ps. 15:1-5; 78:72a;
Prov. 9:10; 10:9; 11:2-3;
Luke 1:74-75; John 8:31-32;
Rom. 12:1-2;
2 Cor. 2:14-17; 3:17-18;
2 Tim. 2:19-21; Jas. 1:2-5

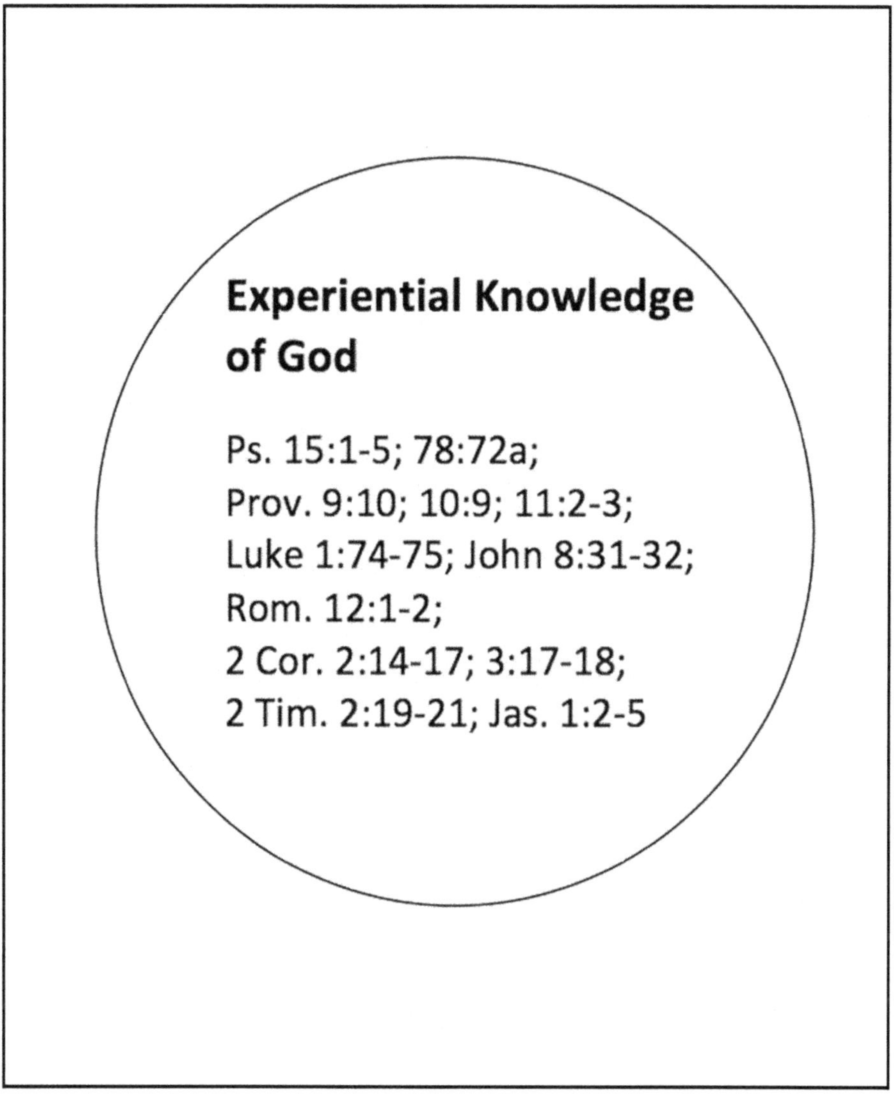

The brother of a young Afghan man had been killed for his Christian faith. The younger brother had resisted the verbal witness of his elder brother and had no intention of investigating Christ further. One night, he had a dream. He found himself in a lush green garden filled with fruit trees. The fruit on the trees looked so luscious, just looking at it made his throat feel dry and parched. But he had no ladder and the trees were too tall for him to reach the fruit. As he tried to think of how to get the delicious-looking fruit, his brother appeared to him in the dream and told him to go to the missionary's home who had worked with him while he was alive. "He will tell you how to get the fruit," his brother told him. That young man came to know Christ and his strong, courageous faith made him a very fruitful evangelist in a hard, dangerous place.[15]

In the West, we can rely too much on the power of our intellect. Perhaps we need to experience God more. In the following passage, the Psalmist describes what an "experiencing God life" can be like:

Lord, who may dwell in your sacred tent?
Who may live on your holy mountain?
He whose walk is blameless and who does what is
righteous, who speaks the truth from his heart
and has no slander on his tongue,
who does his neighbor no wrong
and casts no slur on his fellowman,
who despises a vile man but honors those who

fear the LORD, *who keeps his oath even when
it hurts*, who lends his money without usury
and does not accept a bribe against the innocent.
He who does these things will never be shaken.
(Psalm 15:1-5 NIV, emphasis added)

This Psalm gives us a clear, succinct definition of integrity: one who *keeps his oath even when it hurts*. The Psalmist goes on to unpack the term more: does

---

[15] J. Christy Wilson. *More to Be Desired Gold: A Collection of True Stories Told by Christy Wilson.*

what is right; speaks the truth from his heart; has no slander on his tongue; does no wrong to his neighbor; casts no slur on his fellowman.

Interactive prayer has helped many thousands around the world to have a deeper, more intimate experience with Jesus and walk with greater integrity. Our compulsions and self-defeating ways of thinking and doing can disappear as Jesus keeps His promise, "Whatever you bind on earth will be bound in heaven, and whatever you loose on earth will be loosed in heaven" (Matthew 16:19b; 18:18b NIV).

Experiencing God in this way, not only deepens our love relationship with Jesus, but can be the catalyst for dramatic life change. I know of friends from all over the world who struggled with various compulsions or defeating patterns of thinking, and are now free—because Jesus set them free. Why are Charismatic and Pentecostal churches more open to this type of ministry? Many of the people who have profited from healing prayer come from and now serve with non-Charismatic denominations.

The commitment of our mind is foundational to our growth in Christ. But discipleship must touch the heart in a deep way, and hands in a practical way for our growth to be truly transformational. Experiencing God, deeply and ongoingly, is a key to the heart change that results consistently in disciple multipliers. And times of recurring "spiritual breakthrough" are a consistently reported trait of those who "finish well with Christ."

Ministry & Godly Living Skill Competence

Likewise, teach the older women to be reverent in the way they
live, not to be slanderers or addicted to much wine, but to
teach what is good.
Then they can train the younger women to love their husbands
and children, to be self-controlled and pure, to be busy at
home, to be kind, and to be subject to their husbands, so that
no one will malign the word of God.
Similarly, encourage the young men to be self-controlled.
In everything set them an example by doing what is good. In
your teaching show integrity, seriousness... (Titus 2:3-7 NIV)

We have a believer friend in Japan who has been told on more than one occasion
by non-Christian friends of hers, "I believe your God, now tell me about him."
She is currently leading a growing seeker Bible study with just such friends. But
it didn't start with a Bible study. It started with a woman living an exemplary
life, taking good care of her family, and making serious time for friends in need
in the neighborhood. She definitely "does not eat the bread of idleness" in spite
of advancing years, but still manages to prioritize friendships that often become
redemptive.

If we are to be used redemptively, developing competence in ministry skills
and Godly living is vital. It's unrealistic to think that we will be able to represent
Christ with our family, friends, workplaces, and communities if we are not
equipped to do so. Some churches have taken note of this need and have tried
to equip their people to live a model life and skillfully represent Christ in their
context.

The problem has been that these attempts at equipping often focus on just
informing members. This does not cover the disciple's need to be empowered
and equipped, and therefore, is not an effective way to train folks for service in
the trenches.

Figure 8. Ministry & Godly Living Skill Competence

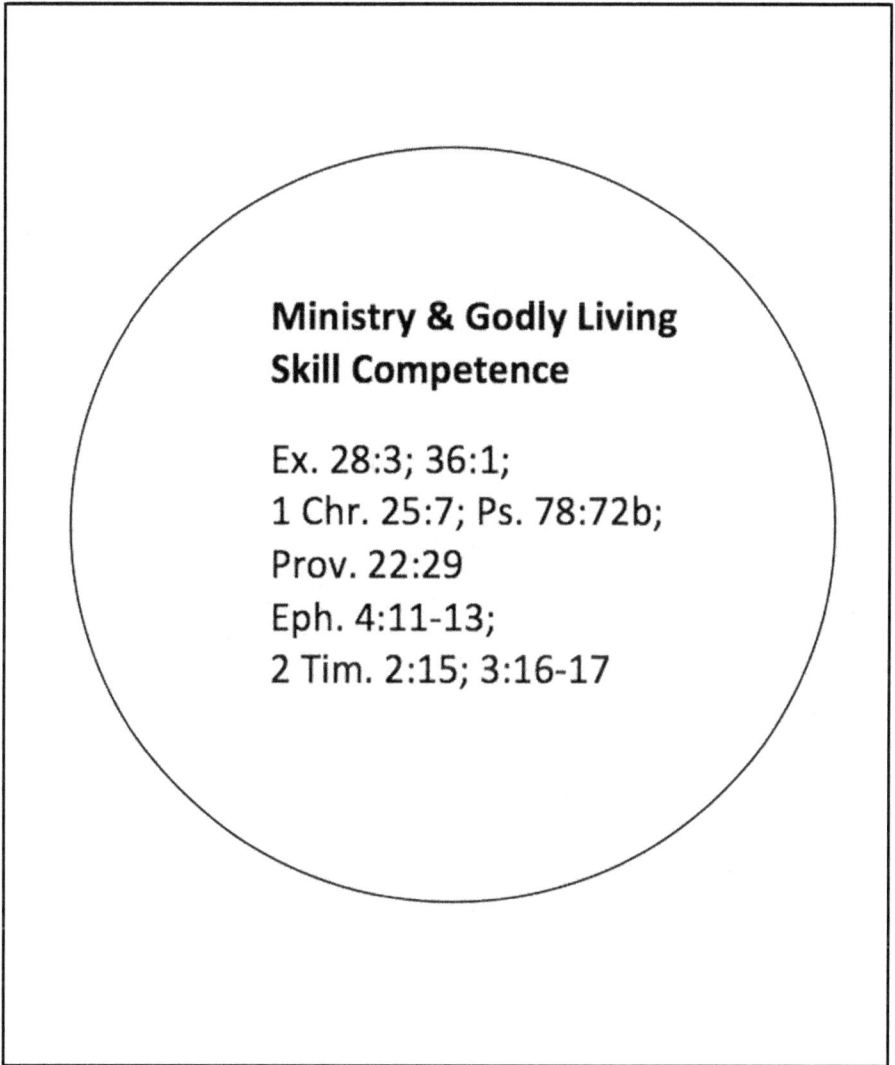

Ministry & Godly Living Skill Competence

Ex. 28:3; 36:1;
1 Chr. 25:7; Ps. 78:72b;
Prov. 22:29
Eph. 4:11-13;
2 Tim. 2:15; 3:16-17

T4T is a disciple training method that is largely responsible for the fact that there are more than 100 million followers of Christ in China today.[16] T4T training includes Pastoral Care, Worship, Accountability, Vision Casting, New Lesson/Bible Study, Practice, and Set Goals and Pray. All seven are important for developing "disciple makers."

Of these seven important components of the training, trainers have found—and a survey by the Gallup business journal confirms[17]—that there are four elements that are non-negotiable keys of effective training that "sticks" for disciple/trainer multiplication:

1) Vision Casting
2) Practice the Lesson
3) Set Goals and Pray
4) Accountability.

Developing skills in living an attractive life in today's environment takes more than just information. Ministry and godly life skills are caught rather than taught most of the time. Mentoring of younger disciples by more experienced Christ followers is a key to developing these transformational competencies of disciple multiplication.

For example, a couple who has traveled a disciple-multiplying road can invest in other couples with whom they find resonance to share some of the wisdom and experience they have acquired. As the friendships deepen, these couples can pray for and encourage one another in living as ambassadors of Christ in their individual contexts—and keep the multiplication going—twofold!

That said, in this technological age, some of us older "Boomers" could use help from younger believers. My young adult daughter has helped me a lot in refining ideas. Her perspective and experiences have helped me to stay aware

---

[16] Steve Smith with Ying Kai. 2011. *T4T: A Discipleship ReRevolution.* p. 144-145.
[17] Craig Kamins. Gallup Business Journal. "How to Make Training a Catalyst for Real Change" (downloaded 3/13/2014 from businessjournal.gallup.com).

of the thoughts and attitudes of today's twenty-somethings, or anyone younger than me.

Some skills have more of a learning component. For example, I know a financial advisor in America's Mid-West who lives an excellent life. Sam works hard, still keeps his family a priority, and obviously loves them all dearly. He does all this while he also serves in many capacities at his church. Here's the really neat thing: For over 20 years, Sam's business has profited from God's serendipitous help. Shunning work-a-holism, Sam seeks God and his Kingdom first, and still succeeds in his business. His partners—all believers—can't understand it. Sam's example of a godly *and effective* life is one that God can use to inspire and guide those of us who are committed to going against the cultural flow to live in radical obedience to Him.

The Church needs gifted teachers and mentors like Sam who can share their successful experiences practically living out the Word of God in the business world, the educational world, the athletic world, the home maker's world, and so on. As Paul himself wrote, "Therefore I urge you to imitate me" (1 Cor. 4:15 NIV).

In some alternative Christian communities, it is common for those who have done something well to share their practical knowledge with those who are less experienced—"apprentices", if you will. This relational help is precious for a young man or woman struggling with something too big for them alone and in need of a mentor.

As we prioritize both building into others and being built up, we are involved in the great mission of the Church. We will go a long way towards creating a culture that leads to disciple multiplication in our churches. The relational skills gained in the process will equip us to be empathetic multiplying disciples ourselves as we get out into whatever "world" the Lord has placed us for his glory.

Scripture Knowledge with Application

"The grass withers and the flowers fall, but the word of our
God stands forever."
(Isaiah 40:8 NIV)

"Is not my word like fire," declares the LORD, "and like a
hammer that breaks a rock in pieces?"
(Jeremiah 23:29 NIV)

The Word of God is faithful and powerful beyond our comprehension. After
thousands of years, the truths of the Bible remain stronger than ever. The Word
will never change but how we deliver it must change when the worldview of the
people around us changes significantly.

The Bible is more than just abstract truth. James tells us we need to be
doers of the Word and not just hearers for it to do us any good (Jas. 1:22-25).
The Lord Jesus used the analogy of two builders (Matt. 7:24-27). The wise one
builds on the Rock and the foolish builds on the sand. The differentiating factor
is whether or not one puts the Word of God into practice. We do not know the
Word if we have just heard it or read it. We come to know it as we apply it and
experience God in the process.

Jesus says the ones who put His words into practice truly love him. Frank
C. Laubach, who was used by God to bring millions to Christ through a literacy
program in the Philippines and Africa, wrote in his diary,

> "Knowing God better and better is an achievement of
> friendship. When two persons fall in love there may be such
> a strong feeling of fellowship, such a delight in the friend's
> presence, that one may lose oneself in the deepening discovery
> of another person.
> The self and the person loved become equally real.
> There are, therefore, three questions which we may ask: 'Do

you believe in God?' That is not getting very far. 'The devils believe and tremble.' Second, 'Are you acquainted with God?' We are acquainted with people with whom we have had some business dealings. Third, 'Is God your friend?' or putting this another way, "Do you love God?"[18]

---

[18] Frank Charles Laubach. 1964. *Frank Laubach's Prayer Diary.* p. 76 of 98.

Figure 9. Scripture Knowledge with Application

Scripture Knowledge
with Application

Ps. 119:89-105;
Matt. 7:24-27;
2 Cor. 2:14-16;
Eph. 4:13-14;
2 Tim. 2:15, 3:15-17;
Heb. 4:12; James 1:22-25

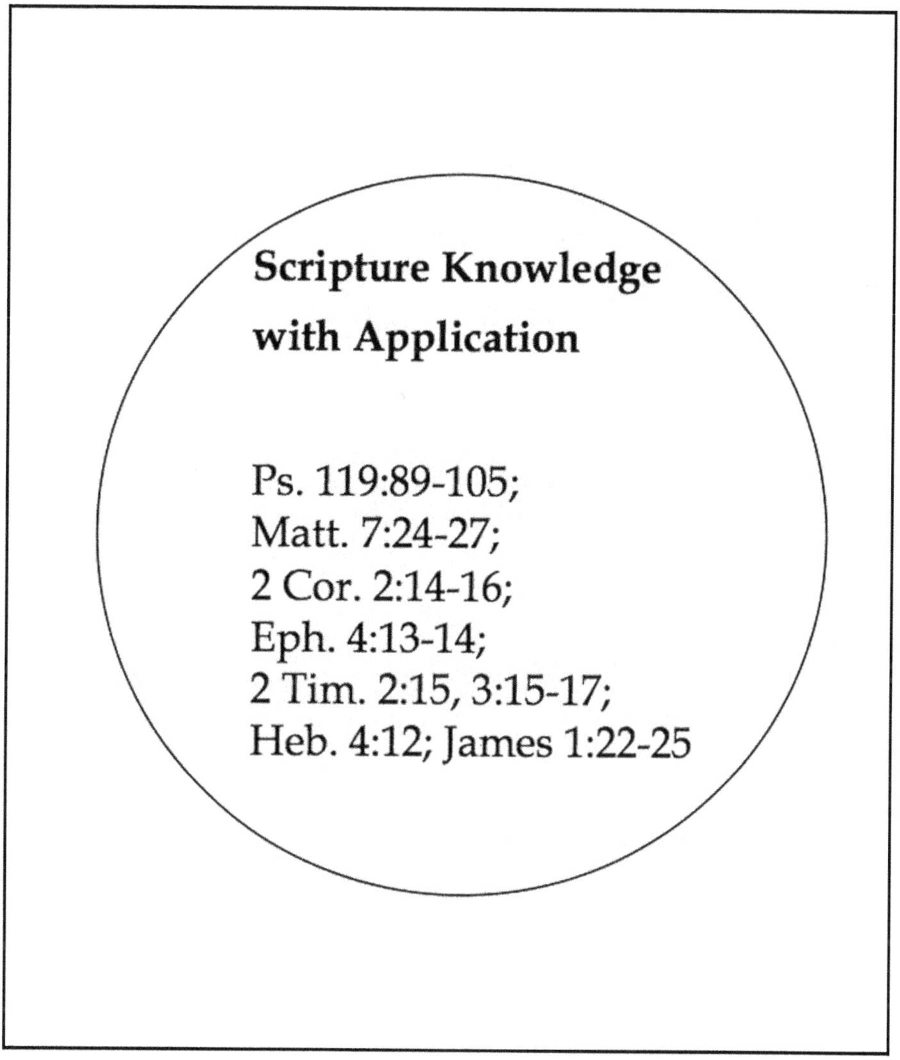

We need to not only know, but *obey* the Word to be considered Christ's close friend (John 14:15, 21, 23). If we want answered prayer, we cannot pick and choose, but need to put all of His Word into practice and cooperate with Holy Spirit (John 15:7). This is, of course, according to our ability based on our maturity in Christ. His grace covers the rest!

I believe "remaining or abiding" in Christ (John 14 and 15) is synonymous with "keeping in step" with the Spirit (Galatians 5:25). What this means is we need the Spirit's help to live out what we read in the Word in order to be obedient.

Gaining this kind of Scripture knowledge, and then the motivation and means with which to apply it to our life, begins with the commitment to regular, personal time with God and His Word. As we commit to this time, how we approach it can be vital to its value.

Discovery Learning is an approach that can help us both in devotional reading of the Word and more serious study for self or others. The great thing about discovery learning is there's a built-in motivation to live it out—and to tell others about it.

Journaling is an effective method of discovery Bible learning. We can spend time reflecting on the previous day as we reflect on the Word we've read (if we're journaling in the morning) or on our just-completed day (if journaling in the evening). Then, write out a prayer in our diary in response to our reflection. Is there something I need to confess? Or is there something I should do to bring restoration? Is there a blessing I want to celebrate? Once I write the appropriate prayer and pray it, I can wait with pen or pencil in hand for God to say something to me in response. His responses can cluster around a theme unique to anyone of us. He reassures and affirms his precious children who seek his heart. And he never tires of telling us how much He loves us in new, affectionate, and sometimes even humorous ways.

There are many good resources for devotional Bible study but I would caution against a steady diet of pre-digested devotionals from experts. That's just lazy and keeps our own interpretive muscles from developing. It betrays thinking that says, "I just need special information to grow in Christ." Remember, the goal of personal devotions is connecting with God—and he is waiting!

To develop a base of scripture knowledge that helps in Bible interpretation and recognizing the voice of Jesus, reading four chapters a day in the Bible will get us through the whole book in one year. While that may sound daunting at first, reading at least this much Scripture will flood our brains with enough Truth to counter the barrage of lies we hear continuously from our media culture. This is my own preferred devotional Bible study method.

Unfortunately many, especially in evangelical churches, have had a steady diet of primarily cognitive Bible study for years—even decades. I sometimes help such brothers and sisters "detox" by sending them one of the links online to "*lectio divina*" Bible study (see Appendix IV). Many friends in this boat do not think they can hear the still, small voice of God, but journaling with reflection on the day can help us unstop our spiritual ears and so can lectio divina.

Another key tool to discovery learning that results in obedience to the Word is *learning the Word in community.* Studying the Bible together enables us to reflect and teach one another from our collective insights. This gives us the building blocks with which to apply the truths of Scripture to our lives in practical ways.

Research has shown that when information is received by lecture, only 5% of it is retained after 24 hours.[19] Information received through group discussion, if done well, is retained at a rate of 50%. If there is an opportunity to put the information into practice within 24 hours, 75% of the information is retained. When learners teach each other after a time of reflection, the average retention rate approximates 90%. And when that is followed up by immediate use of the learning in real life, **there is close to 100% retention.**

---

[19] David Sousa. *How the Brain Learns.* (2005) ISBN 0-7619-7765-1.

Jeff Reed is author of a small group curriculum called *Church Based Theological Education (CBTE)*. To use his small group curriculum, we will need to "raise the bar on what it means to be a disciple," especially for those who have been "spoon fed" for a long time. In *Teaching the First Principles*, he states:

> What makes *The First Principles Series* unique? It uses a
> very different approach from other contemporary attempts
> at training believers in the basics of the faith. It draws on
> significantly different educational methods to ensure that the
> learning experiences produce thinking Christians, solid in their
> faith (p. 7) (Reed, 2003).[20]

CBTE has been translated into many languages. Sometimes they require some cultural adaptation for maximum effect overseas. At our house church in Okinawa, we used CBTE in a small-group study. After a short time, one dear lady with little formal education who had been a believer for over a year became convinced that she wanted to be baptized. The way she realized it (discovery learning) motivated her to move on (apply) that realization immediately. She multiplied when she invited her adult daughter to our ALPHA Course. Her daughter also came to believe Christ and was baptized.

CBTE is an example of how individual reflection and peer teaching in community can be utilized for "truth discovery." A concept or question is introduced to the group after reading the Word together, and each attender reflects on that concept or question and notes their reflections. They process the material in a time of individual reflection and consulting selected passages in reference books. This is then followed by a time of teaching one another—peer teaching. If time is taken and learners can be fully engaged—often "detoxing" is necessary for learners who have had a steady diet of lecture or other "spoon feeding" (cf. Appendix IV)—then a second round of individual reflection can be implemented for more polished applications.

---

[20] Jeff Reed. *Teaching the First Principles*. (2003) ISBN 1-891441-09-4.

Through this type of study, members think through principles and concepts more thoroughly and often discover new insights they are eager to apply. They are often encouraged for their hard work of reflecting and bringing their findings to the group.

This kind of discovery learning is hard work for the unaccustomed, but carries within it a built-in motivation to apply what we have learned in real life experience. As discoverers, we own our insights. Perhaps someone could have told us the same thing, but it would not have had the same power to motivate us to apply it to our lives. This kind of learning is transformational and contributes powerfully to a culture of disciple multiplication in a church.

11
BETTER THAN ACCEPTABLE RECOVERY

In our first church planting assignment in Tokyo, we worked with a wonderful holiness church, Nerima Grace Chapel, to develop a daughter church. We believed that God was calling us to plant churches at approximately thirty-minute intervals on the Seibu-Ikebukuro train line. Kiyose, about thirty minutes up the train line from Nerima, seemed ideal for the first phase of the plan to be implemented. At the mother church, Nerima Grace Pastor Ogasawara commissioned four cell groups to launch the initial new church in the plan.

I had worked with Nerima church members for a year and a half in both evangelism and in how to conduct the on-the-job training of prospective church planting team members. As the time came to shift attention to development of the new church, we focused outreach in the community of Kiyose.

Because so many housewives attended the new-church gatherings without their husbands, I made it a point to try and meet and befriend these husbands. Having come from an alcoholic family of origin myself, my motivation to build strong Christ-centered marriages in the new church was perhaps greater than usual. I developed a curriculum for outreach ministry to these church widows and their workaholic husbands. Scheduling was difficult and the men were reluctant to spend what little free time they had at a church function.

What worked best was to spend time with the husbands individually. As our friendship grew, I was able to share some of the blessings of having a living relationship with a Living Savior and having a "triple-braided marriage" (Ecclesiastes 4:12).

As these men overcame their avoidance of church and church people, some came to Christ, or their priorities shifted enough that we could invite them to "Couple Time" gatherings, where we worked on increased communication and intimacy in their marriages.

God worked on the marriages of the men and women who came. For the first time, husbands and wives began sitting together in church. We heard good testimonies of increased communication and even an occasional "date night." We praised God for the reconciliation and salvation that seemed to be happening.

Unfortunately, there was a blow-up as we prepared to leave Japan for a home assignment. One couple that had been married 38 years was experiencing quite a bit of conflict with the new level of communication, and none of us felt equipped to help them resolve things. In addition, one troubled lady started calling us late at night and loudly scolding us for what she perceived were shortcomings in our work with them.

While our relational outreach ministry had produced much fruit, we did not have the prayer resources to deal with the stresses created by the very fruit being produced in the ministry. Things get "messy" when people start dealing with real issues in community. The church that gets involved in frontlines outreach in a pantheistic or post-Christian culture must have systems in place to bring new people into contact with the healing grace of Jesus.

With these issues unresolved, we returned to the States for a nine-month home assignment. Staying with friends in Evansville, we learned that our hosts had recently received training in a prayer tool called *Theophostic*—meaning "God's light." It turned out to be the resource we wished we could have had back in Japan.

Dr. Ed Smith, developer of *Theophostic* prayer, had been counseling rape and incest victims for years and had become dissatisfied with what he characterized as "just tolerable recovery" after years of counseling. Smith, a pastor as well as counselor, searched the scriptures and became convinced that Jesus wanted to do more to help those he counseled than psychology alone could provide.

The result was *Theophostic* prayer—a ministry tool that has helped Christians around the world to overcome the debilitating lies they believe. I can personally testify that when the Lord's healing hand touched me through Theophostic prayer, it was like Christ removed "stress buttons" in my life. I have heard similar testimonies from cross-cultural missionaries working on a number of continents.

We have all experienced situations that can compel us to react in ways that do not honor God. The result of Theophostic prayer (and some others) is that I am less reactive in stressful situations and am able to exhibit the fruit of the Spirit more consistently in my life with Christ. If I'm honest here, I must confess that without the grace of God through the prayer methods I mention in this book, I believe I would be dead or in prison right now instead of serving my King and Master Jesus.

Since that time in Indiana, I have also experienced two other valuable prayer tools: *Restoring the Foundations* and *Releasing Prayer Ministry*. Here I briefly repeat what I shared on pages 28-30: *Restoring the Foundations* helps Christians deal with the four obstacles we face in our quest to finish the race well with Christ:

> 1) Generational curse (Exodus 5:20)
> 2) Ungodly beliefs (John 8:31-32)
> 3) Wounds of the heart (Psalm 34:18) which often result in
>   unforgiveness (Matthew 6:14-15)
> 4) Demonic oppression (Matthew 18:33-35; Luke 8:2)

Resources for the *Theophostic*[21] and *Restoring the Foundations*[22] prayer methodology resources are listed in the bibliography and links to their webpages are footnoted at the bottom of this page. There would be far fewer moral failures in the Church if this kind of inner healing ministry were more common in the church. Church counseling services that offered this type of prayer ministry—in addition their counseling—to anyone who volunteers could see many seekers and believers set free of compulsions and neurotic fears as well as trauma that often resists regular counseling.

Theophostic prayer is most helpful with people who have been severely traumatized. The systematic approach of *Restoring the Foundations* is well suited to generational curse issues including elimination of illicit vows or unclean sexual ties.

---

[21] Dr. Ed Smith. Theophostic Prayer Ministry. **http://www.theophostic.com/**

[22] Chester and Betsy Kylstra. *Restoring the Foundations*. Video: **http://www.restoringyourlife.org/**

Yet another prayer tool I would like to introduce here is *Releasing Prayer Ministry* (RPM) developed by Evergreen Baptist Church in San Gabriel Valley, California. It is designed to help believers develop intimacy with Jesus, including more sensitivity to hearing his voice. Evergreen, an Asian-descent congregation that has sent many teams to work with us in Japan, uses RPM in their discipleship.

More than one Japanese church we have worked with in Japan has asked me if Evergreen could send one of their members back for a year to help them improve their discipleship. They want to produce the empowered, empathic, capable, believers with character like the ones who have come over from Evergreen on short-term teams.

It is time for the Church of Jesus Christ to start fighting darkness with both hands. Prayer tools like *Theophostic* Prayer, *Restoring the Foundations*, and *Releasing Prayer Ministry* can help us do just that. On the last page of the body of this book, I provide links for a number of ministry resources including *Releasing Prayer Ministry* (Appendix I #1).

News Flash: After preaching on 2 Cor. 5:14-21) at the Kiyose church in Tokyo in late 2013 using some translated figures from this book and introducing them to *Releasing Prayer Ministry* (cf. Appendix I #1), the church is experiencing amazing revival with dozens of baptisms already, and it just seems to keep on with baptisms scheduled throughout 2014 (remember, this is Japan, I am writing about). Plans are in place to follow through on the original vision to plant churches at approximately thirty-minute intervals on the local train line.

My prayer is that God's people will humble and consecrate themselves to his process of transformation in themselves and their churches so that God's grace might flow freely again and lost souls might find the love and grace they hunger for, and the transformation of self and society that we all so desperately need.

12

CULTURE CHANGE: CHURCH & BEYOND

"Repentance is an attitude rather than a single act."
- Richard Owen Roberts[23]

"Congress proclaimed days of fasting and of thanksgiving annually throughout the Revolutionary War. A proclamation by Congress set May 17, 1776, as a 'day of Humiliation, Fasting and Prayer' throughout the colonies. Congress urged its fellow citizens to 'confess and bewail our manifold sins and transgressions, and by a sincere repentance and amendment of life, appease his [God's] righteous displeasure, and through the merits and mediation of Jesus Christ, obtain his pardon and forgiveness'"[24]

How far our culture has moved...from together seeking Almighty God's forgiveness to a focus on individual entitlement.

In 2013, I heard a strong message on the connection between corporate repentance, spiritual revival, and cultural transformation by Pastor Keith Robinson in Evansville, IN. I've seen this principal at work on both sides of the ocean and believe it is a universal principle.

I pray that we Western Christians can begin to regularly repent on behalf of, and pray for, our leaders. If we are to be cultural change agents, this is vital. I believe this is what the inspired Chronicler (2 Chron. 7:14 NIV) was writing about when he penned:

> if my people who are called by my name, will humble themselves and pray and seek my face and turn from their wicked ways, then I will hear from heaven, and I will forgive their sin and will heal their land.

---

[23] Bruce Wilkinson. (2006) *30 Days to Experiencing Spiritual Breakthroughs.* Kindle location 512-21.

[24] Pray for America National Bus Tour **http://commit2pray.com/a-call-to-prayer/**

The flow of the gospel in Acts is organic and grassroots. That flow continues today. As we humble ourselves daily in repentance and a renewed will to obey, the indwelling Spirit alerts us to specific ways we can join God in his redemptive work in our local context.

This dynamic becomes a display case of God's redemptive grace to others. They are increasingly convicted as they see God working around them, compassionately and powerfully, to redeem any who will taste the Lord's goodness.

This is especially true in Islamic countries, where persecution against believers can erupt into violence at any moment. There are several documented cases of churches in such environments growing dramatically as Christians continue to love and reach out compassionately even as their radical Muslim neighbors are burning Christians' homes—sometimes with the residents still inside.

I've already shared about the Egyptian believers who are winning their enemies to Christ through otherworldly love. In Jakarta, Indonesia one church has grown to 45,000 as a result of Christians continuing to reach out compassionately to their Muslim neighbors even as fiery persecution is carried out against them. Where sin does abound grace does that much more abound (Romans 5:20). God confirms his love for persecutor and persecuted alike by giving many signs and wonders in such a context.

This "God dynamic" is developing among fashion workers in Tokyo. New believers are privileged to discover a God who not only loves them, but also desires an intimate relationship with them through prayer (cf. Appendix I #1 *Releasing Prayer Ministry*). It all started with one who prayed with another who heard from God and believed. Together they listen to God and study the Bible one-to-one. Recently two more believed in Jesus. Together, the four are praying and reaching out to other workers in Tokyo's fashion district.

Salvation occurs as onlookers gradually decide to imbibe of the "God intoxication" that they have seen in their friends. God mysteriously sustains those of his who are struggling even as material success remains elusive (Matt 6:33). As people switch life paradigms and bask in the Lord's goodness, it is natural to recommend this life to others.

Still another example of simple church illustrates the power of community. The *community of the called out* is a friendly Bible study over tea in the inviting home of the hostess who hosts us every time we come to Okinawa. In answer to this dear sister's prayers, this warm and growing community has drawn her new daughter-in-law to Jesus. The group increases as lost and hungry souls are drawn to the warm and inviting fellowship.

The development of "new wineskin" fellowships like these are a vital, culturally-friendly way that God can enfold the harvest he is raising up in each generation and in each locale. Provision in the form of new wineskin *ecclesia*—where heaven meets earth and angels ascend and descend (Genesis 28:12ff)--must be made for those who hunger and thirst for personal transformation, but are turned off by existing church culture.

Another "new wineskin" that will transform our ability to be multipliers is to repent of denominational and theological divisions.

These are often unnecessary stumbling blocks to people who are sincerely looking for a God of love. We represent Him well as we accept all who seek to follow Christ, regardless of their starting point or different points of view on secondary issues.

There is no revival without repentance, and repentance releases God's grace but pride results in his opposition (James 4:6, 1 Peter 5:5). Blackaby and King in *Fresh Encounter* define revival as "a divinely initiated work in which God's people pray, repent of their sin, and return to a holy, Spirit-filled, obedient, love relationship with God."[25] Repentance comes when God changes us. The spiritually deadening impediment of sin must be dealt with and taken away. While we have been saved by faith in Christ, the stain of our sin can still block the flow of God's presence and power in our lives. Without holiness, no one will see God (Hebrews 12:14).

As the Kiyose church we planted was becoming established, the Lord gave us several salvations in a short span of time. In consultation with the mother church elders, we decided that it would be good to take a few established church

---

[25] Henry & Richard Blackaby & Claude King. *Fresh Encounter: God's Pattern for Spiritual Awakening* (2009). p. 15.

members along with these new believers on a short-term mission trip to exercise the latter's "newbie enthusiasm" and give them a cross-cultural opportunity to trust God and see him work in unfamiliar settings. We planned to send the team to work with a dynamic church in Taichung, Taiwan.

For four consecutive Sundays leading up to the trip, our team of 10 Japanese believers, their Japanese co-leader, and me (the lone expatriate) met after church to prepare for the trip. The team was made up of roughly half new believers and half church members who had led them to faith in Christ. Excitement was high and we laughed a lot over the lunch of curry rice we enjoyed together during the meetings.

The time came and we flew to Taichung for the ten-day mission. After the first day, my Japanese co-leader came to me and said, "Mike, we are sensing that the pastor here is not comfortable with us (Japanese). When we come into the room, he can hardly wait to leave." We discovered that the pastor had been raised by grandparents who had been tortured and killed by the Japanese military during World War II.

After reflection and prayer, our team co-leader suggested to both the team and me that he and the other Japanese team members perform a foot washing ceremony for the church as a public act of group repentance. He asked me if I would represent the American people. He also asked a mainland Chinese leader who was there at the same time to represent the Chinese people who suffered, and that the oldest member of the local church represent the Taiwanese people. While I admit to being uncomfortable, I felt like this was something from God that I should not resist.

Later that morning, the church's 400 members came in and filled the worship hall. The pastor was sitting in the front row. The old grandma from the membership, the Chinese team leader and myself were all seated in a row on the dais. There was little talk as the room filled.

The door opened slowly; my co-leader crawled in with his face very close to the floor. The Japanese team members all followed—close to the floor and weeping loudly.

Everyone watching in the room was absolutely silent. First, the team came to me, removed my socks and proceeded to wash my feet—you could've heard a pin drop. The team then moved to the Chinese team leader and began to wash her feet. When the sobbing team got to the grandma, the sobbing spread to everyone else in the room. As they washed the grandma's feet, wails were heard. There was not a dry eye in the place.

After that day, the pastor was different. He wanted to be with the team and would hug my co-leader in greeting. The pastor opened doors for our witness in city offices and the largest hospital in town-- with 72 coming to faith in Christ in over just nine days. And since this powerful time 15 years ago, the two churches have maintained and nurtured their relationship, exchanging short-term missionaries at least once a year. That public act of contrition changed the culture of both churches. No one involved has been the same since.

Corporate repentance changes hearts. I wonder what God would do if a substantial number of North American churches took one Sunday a month to engage in a humble and public act of repentance? Could it be that the Almighty would begin to turn the hearts of this nation back to himself (2 Chronicles 7:14)?

13
THREE MULTIPLIER CASE STUDIES

If I may say so, when we lead a soul to Christ, we lead but one. When, however, like Joshua of old, we are able to lead a saint into the land that flows with milk and honey, we are the means of saving a thousand. The soul thus empowered becomes another Joshua, a center of light and blessing and power, and himself a winner of souls. (Wilkes, 1944) (p. 132).

If you do not already know someone, typically Christians need to make friendship deposits before initiating spiritual dialogue. It helps when the person feels comfortable with you relationally. Building relationship requires you to:

- Be a genuine friend
- Listen intently
- Connect along interest areas
- Invest time
- Show how you care
- Share your life (appropriately)
- Use disclosure to deepen the bonds
- Sustain momentum

An ongoing committed relationship is essential for influence because when you talk to someone "once in a blue moon" you do not create necessary relational trust, dialogue, spiritual example, and prayer focus. Two wings make the evangelistic process fly:

Committed Relationship ←→ *Spiritual Dialogue*

(Comer, 2013, p. 154)

This chapter introduces three evangelistic multipliers. Considered together, these vignettes offer examples of what is possible when ordinary believers like you and me, compelled by Christ's love, take it upon ourselves to follow Christ into the harvest. Holy adventure awaits each who will risk to be obedient to Jesus.

Yuko (Office Worker): Marketplace Evangelism

I was born in Naha, the prefectural capital of Okinawa, Japan. I am the second of four daughters. My father is a carpenter and my mother is a housewife. Both are now believers so there was no problem giving up the family altar (*butsudan*) or any of the associated rituals.

I'm not married. I started working in an office after high school graduation. I was given the opportunity to receive technical training in my company and have risen to leadership in the office.

My greatest joy at work or anywhere I go is to tell anyone I encounter how wonderful it is to walk with Jesus day by day. Christ has done so much for me, and he often reminds me of just the right thing to mention when I am talking with someone.

God has given me the joy of leading eight people to Christ. Most of these are not only colleagues at work, but very good friends. I was able to develop a trust relationship with each one that helped in leading them to Christ. Several of them have since led others to Christ.

In my spare time, I like to engage in flower arranging, crafts, cooking, and caring for children at church events. My church trains all of us in how to share our faith with others using an evangelistic Bible study the pastor developed. The most fun I have is when I share how God is blessing me and that leads to the other person putting their trust in Christ.

❧

Yuko's effervescent joy is infectious. She is so positive and cheerful that she lifts up those around her. Truly, the joy of the Lord is her strength and rivers of living water flow out of her innermost being pretty much continually. As a result, God has made her exceptionally fruitful.

While we may not be gifted just like Yuko, we are told that good soil produces a multiplied harvest. This process involves each one of us who "gossips the gospel", scattering seeds of testimony wherever we go. Our Spirit-filled presence nurtures such seed and helps move a spiritual harvest to maturity.

As we abide in Christ, the joy of the Lord becomes our very present strength and "infects" others as we interact at work, in the neighborhood or in our family.

Koshi (Business Executive): A Valuable Exception

I am currently executive of a Corporation focused on developing a nationwide digital network. From its inception for many years I managed this operation directly. Now I supervise the ones who manage it.

Fifteen years ago, my doctor told me I needed to take up tennis again for my health. About the same time I met Jack, who accepted my invitation to play regularly. We played most Saturday mornings for two years. We drank a lot of tea together and also played chess and shogi (a Japanese game similar to chess). Whenever we would get together, Jack would tell me some way God had blessed his life. Little by little, my interest in his God grew.

One time, the day before we were to play tennis, there was a family crisis that left me very worried. Between games the next day, Jack told me about a similar crisis that had occurred in his family, and how using principles in the Bible, God had helped them to resolve the situation right away. I wanted to hear more and eagerly accepted his invitation to join a men's cell group he was forming.

My wife had been a Christian for many years before me. During that time, I occasionally heard her pastor's sermon tapes, saw a Christian TV show, heard Christian music, read a Christian book, or attended a Christian wedding. All these contacts with gospel influences gradually changed me.

Finally, the men's cell group Jack invited me to became a good group of friends for me—something I had not had for a long time. Through an inductive Bible study, I understood John chapter one for the first time. When Jack told me one day he wanted me to be his spiritual brother, I gladly accepted the idea and prayed with him to accept Christ as my Savior.

After Jack and his family moved away, I became part of another cell group. Our members had a number of barbeques, dinners, book discussions, and game nights on a rotating basis to which we invited unsaved friends. I invited several men and their wives from my work. At these gatherings, we would share little snippets of how our lives were being blessed by God—not sermons—but little bits of "holy gossip."

Within a year, six couples from my and other members' workplaces believed in Christ through these activities and were baptized. In addition, I have led two people to Christ who have gone on to lead other people to Christ.

❧

Koshi has led two people to Christ who have multiplied by leading others to the Savior. Koshi and his wife's active outreach and sharing of blessings have inspired others to ask their unsaved friends to consider Christ. Koshi's willingness to share Christ in the workplace and in partnership with other willing believers has resulted in many new members in at least two different churches.

Nate (Heating & A/C technician who plays the background)

Nate came to Christ as a young adult. There was a mini-revival in his neighborhood and he was reached by a new church fellowship in the area. For ten years, the church enjoyed health and growth; then the church began to falter as the pastor's influence outgrew his character and his unresolved personal issues created dysfunctional patterns in the church community that could be seen by others.

The church's dysfunction really frustrated Nate. He tried talking with the pastor and elders. He was even an elder himself for a while. However, he could see that the church was consistently drifting from the Word of God. No new people were being won for Christ. The young people left church, and their faith, once they got to high school.

Nonetheless, Nate persevered in sharing his faith with his co-workers and others in his neighborhood. Even though he gave out hundreds of tracts and was not shy about witnessing, no one he talked with ever showed any inclination to believe.

One summer during the annual church overnight camp and picnic, Nate was in the facility's public bath with a new missionary. He was a little surprised when the Spirit seemed to nudge him to sit down next to the missionary who promptly asked him, "Do you want to work with me to plant a new church?"

Nate found the thought exciting. His excitement spurred him on to pray about the new ministry. As he prayed the conviction grew in him that this was something he would like to have a part in. Nate was more than ready to say, "Yes!"

This started a most exciting adventure for Nate and his wife Judy. With the missionary couple, they went to an ALPHA Course training at a nearby Catholic church. Nate was surprised because the priest preached a passionate and compelling gospel message as a preamble to the training. "Hey," Nate thought, "I guess Catholics can be brothers and sisters in Christ too."

Nate, his wife, the missionary, and his wife decided to start an ALPHA Course at the missionaries' home. Nate enthusiastically passed out flyers to anybody and everybody he could. Nate asked co-workers, folks in the neighborhood, and old friends from his baseball playing days.

One of his friends visited the first ALPHA Course but dropped out. However, his friend came back to the second Course, and eventually accepted Christ at the third Course. A banker friend of Nate's came to the third Course and later accepted Christ.

While Nate has never personally led anyone to Christ, he is a multiplier. People he invited or encouraged along the way have not only believed for themselves, but have also reached others. Nate "got into the game" and will share in heavenly rewards someday, when Christ receives him home.

14

A MANY-LAYERED CAKE

Christian multipliers come to Christ in many ways. However, there are always three common factors. They come to believe through *the Word of God—both spoken and modeled.* They come to faith in the context of *a warm, accepting relationship.* Finally, there is *a crisis in the life of the future multiplier* that opens their heart to first considering Christ and then receiving him as Savior into their life.

It usually takes many layers of witness for someone to believe. There will usually have been gospel seeds scattered, gentle waterings, and finally a timely harvester to reap the fruit of another soul snatched from destruction and brought into life. Witness is usually a lot like a wood block painting like the Japanese paintings of Mt. Fuji or a fishing village. The paint is applied painstakingly layer upon layer with wood blocks until we behold the masterpiece.

I once heard a man upon his decision to be baptized recount 23 different contacts with the gospel on the way to him finally believing—and this is just how many he could remember after several years of the Lord pursuing him!

Research shows that Christian pre-schools, Sunday school, VBS, Christian movies, Christian music, Christian novels and other books, Christian concerts, funerals, and weddings can all play a part in laying down layers of witness that later bear fruit. Other multipliers have shared how taped messages, testimonies they heard, mysterious feelings and encounters with God—with one multiplier, an audible voice—prepared them for a timely invitation to Christian commitment.

An important factor to consider is whether or not the person we are trying to reach has spiritual ears to hear or not. In a post-Christian culture like the USA or Canada, or a pantheistic culture like Japan, most people we encounter do not yet have spiritual ears to hear the gospel—the distance from what they hear every day to biblical truth is just too great. For them, we must come as a friendly, loving messenger. We help them as we can. As our friendship with them deepens, we can offer to pray for them. As they receive answers to our prayers, many will develop ears to hear a more direct gospel message—aimed at their point of perceived need.

Often our unsaved friend will have an openness to a friendly messenger long before they are open to Bible study or entering a church.

15
TAKE-OUT GOSPEL

In my study of disciple multiplication, nearly every multiplier I studied made it
their habit to share the gospel at work, in their neighborhood, or at their friend's
home.

The context for witnessing that results in multiplication is *always* relational.
There is a transference of evangelistic passion that takes place in a relationship
that includes trust, acceptance, and fun. And always remember the benefits
of just hanging out. Spending time with an unsaved friend on their turf is
never wasted time. Whether they eventually believe in Christ or not, they will
experience the love of Christ through you as you exhibit acceptance, kindness,
and gentleness. And just maybe, God will bring a spiritual harvester to your
friend in a time of harvest as the spiritual seeds you planted mature.

We have used the *Releasing Prayer Ministry* for building intimacy between
God and his servants, but also to minister to grieving non-Christians after a
disaster. Several accepted Christ as they sensed his great compassion for them
during prayer. A witness who can facilitate an unbelieving friend to "experience
our compassionate, loving God" can often be much more effective than one
who can only recite memorized Bible verses that the unbeliever has no ability to
understand yet. If such a believer can approach the newcomer relationally, there
can well come a time when their memorized scripture can be powerfully put
into play.

As we are transformed by God's grace, his love will increasingly compel
us to become *ambassadors of reconciliation* between Christ and people (2 Cor.
5:14-21). An ambassador goes to the people. This is where they have the
greatest credibility and where it is easiest to build a trust relationship—both key
characteristics of disciple multiplication.

16
IN YOU I TRUST

A universal principle of disciple multiplication is that the time spent building trust in a relationship is always worthwhile. For one who would live as an emissary of the King of Kings, it is good to be mindful of Marvin Mayers' Prior Question of Trust: *Is what I'm saying, doing or thinking building or undermining trust?*[26] Another key issue is prioritizing time. Can some TV time be cut? Can some recreation time include some interaction time with newcomers?

The cultural distance between the current North American worldview and a biblical worldview has become so great that most people cannot relate to the idea of a monotheistic God. Therefore, most people you meet will not initially have the spiritual ears to be able to hear the gospel. This is one reason why relational evangelism built on trusting relationships is especially powerful.

Taking the time to develop genuine trust gives the witness more credibility than any other single factor. This developing trust is also the greatest antidote to the common objection we are trying to "sell" something. Even though building trust takes time, the quality of the relationship we will develop, and the fruit it can bear in the life of our unsaved friend, is more than worth the effort. And in the long run multiplied witness is much *faster* than individual witness or program witness that gives unbelievers a "light dusting" of the gospel that most often does not "stick."

[26] Marvin K. Mayers (1987). *Christianity Confronts Culture: A Strategy for Crosscultural Evangelism.* p. 4-15.

17

FISHING "IN HOUSE"

I know of multipliers who have been intentional about attending church outreach events of many kinds in order to develop redemptive friendships with newcomers who come to the events. To be successful, they must be intentional about their purpose, and committed to the long haul. The goal is to develop authentic, *mutually-supportive* friendships with the newcomers. Then, faith can be shared most naturally and compellingly.

My research of evangelistic multipliers indicates that most multipliers reach out to their non-Christian friends and family on their turf. However, there are some multipliers who multiply by proactively attending church events with the intent to form redemptive friendships that develop a life of their own outside of church.

One of these "in house" fishers did not start sharing Christ with anyone until about five years after she was herself baptized. She did not see herself as an evangelist. However, a family tragedy and supernatural healing gave her a newfound passion to share the wonder of the Prince of Peace she knows intimately. She has now multiplied three times and counting!

Other multipliers started sharing the wonderful things they were learning about Christ with other friends before they themselves had yet made a commitment. It is important not to quench the enthusiasm of those who are just "tasting and seeing that the Lord is good." Several started their "careers" as evangelistic multipliers while they themselves were still "seekers."

18

ROLLING WITH THE POWER:
THREE CASE STUDIES

While running the ALPHA Course in Okinawa, God really surprised us. For two years, we had tried several different approaches to plant a new church in Naha, the prefectural capital. After my wife and I undertook the ALPHA Course training along with another couple we were working with, we tried running the course at our apartment.

During the initial running of the course, we had three attenders—a different three every time we met! The second time we ran the course, our numbers increased to 10-12 people. Some previous occasional attenders overcame their fear of religious brain-washing and still others not only adjusted their own schedules so they could attend more regularly, but also invited family members and friends.

The third time we ran ALPHA, our numbers had grown to the point that we were bursting at the seams. The apartment owner kindly helped me find temporary parking for 29 people!

A few weeks into the course, I received a phone call from Mitch, a regular attender. Mitch told me his uncle, a drinker, had fallen from the roof of the family's three-story apartment. He was in the hospital in a coma and the doctors said he would never wake up again. Consistent with Okinawan culture, Mitch's family was consulting a Yuta, an Okinawan shaman. Nonetheless, I assured Mitch we would pray for his uncle and family.

At our next ALPHA meeting, the topic was prayer in Jesus' name, I told the 20+ attenders about Mitch's uncle. One lady who was getting close to belief asked, "Why don't we pray for Mitch's uncle in Jesus' name?" So we did. Many of the prayers were very childlike. Some were praying out loud to the Christian God for the first time in their lives.

A couple of days later, we heard from Mitch that his uncle had astounded his doctors by awakening. He then further astounded everyone present by talking. Within days, he was walking again!

Mitch told us that he believed Jesus had healed his uncle; his family attributed the miraculous turn of events to their consultation with a *Yuta*. But our ALPHA attenders knew that their childlike, first-ever prayers to Christ had been answered. By the end of the course, six attenders had been baptized– some in the ocean, and twelve joined the new church! Most of those were later baptized.

Following are three more multiplier case studies that illustrate how God's miraculous power can work redemptively, outside the bounds of what we normally expect in this modern day and age. Such demonstrations of God's power and concern for people compels them to follow him enthusiastically and naturally recommend him to others.

Henry (Newspaper Reporter):
Have Gospel, Will Travel

I was born in Kansas City to a self-employed businessman and a mother who worked in an office. When I was ten years old, my parents divorced. My father moved out of our home abandoning mother, my younger sister and me. As a result of this, I was never very close to him.

After graduating from university, I married and took a job with a newspaper, and before long I was working as a reporter. The job involved frequent transfers, usually every two years.

Away from work, I'm a private person, though I do enjoy my hobby as an amateur magician. I've never found it hard to make friends and am often asked for advice, although I really don't know why.

My wife became a Christian before me—partly as a result of a family crisis. When she asked me to go to church with her, I agreed to go. The church was crowded, which surprised me. But that was not the biggest surprise that day.

After the service, a man came up and invited me to a men's cell group. Later, he told me that God's Spirit had told him to come over and talk to me—specifically. This really choked me up—that God would care for me so much as to have a stranger approach me and invite me to a group where I would eventually find Jesus.

After a job transfer, my wife and I started attending a church in Atlanta with a strong cell-group ministry. Soon I was made a cell group leader. When the church hosted a black gospel workshop, our cell got involved preparing and passing out handbills in the surrounding neighborhood. When passing out handbills, the other cell members took my lead to strike up conversations with people we encountered. I intuitively realized that developing some positive feeling—a modicum of trust—would increase the probability of the recipient actually attending the workshop.

During and after the workshop, my cell members and I invited our new friends who attended the workshop to barbeques and home parties. As the trust grew between our new friends and us, some of them became open to the gospel. Eventually, so many came to Christ that our cell group multiplied twice.

Around this time, I met a coach for house church networks in the region. What he taught me inspired me to start a house church in a new area after yet another job transfer. During the two years we were in the new area, we planted a house church.

Eventually, I was made bureau chief for the newspaper and transferred to Charlotte. There my wife and I are working to start yet another house church. Some of the people we have led to faith in Christ have led others to Christ. Most scatter seeds of testimony to many they meet in their daily lives as they "gossip their blessings." God gives the increase as we are faithful to play our parts.

In all, four of the people I have led to Christ have led others to Christ. Some of those last have led yet another generation (3rd) to Christ. I will never forget how God reached out to me when I was not even giving him a thought!

Akiko (Divorced Single Mom):
Maintaining Family Ties

When I married, I thought we would have a happy family, but shortly after our first baby was born, my husband abandoned us. I was forced to move back to my parents' home in southern Japan. Soon after, my husband and I divorced.

One day as I was nursing my infant child, I heard a voice say to me, "Re-do your childhood." But I didn't know whose voice it was and I didn't understand the meaning. Soon after, a friend came on the train from far away and shared with me the way to be born again (John 3:3). I understood that it had been Jesus' voice speaking to me! I was baptized in my bathtub the same day. That's my story of meeting Jesus and re-doing my childhood!

❧

Akiko keeps the dialogue going with her animistic parents. She accepts them and gently tries to show them a better way in Christ. As the oldest child, Akiko is expected to make the arrangements for extended family to get together at certain traditional times of the year. Akiko does so but keeps a clear Christian testimony. She makes it clear that she does not expect her ancestors to be able to help or harm her in any way.

Akiko has been able to gather a house church of redeemed friends. This faith community has multiplied more than once through evangelism. There have been times when the house church members have been able to gather around Akiko's parents and pray for them. This has been a positive encounter and the parents seem to be slowly drawing closer to Christ. Akiko continues to pray and show respect as well as she can.

❧

Research suggests that in order for a Christian to stay engaged with non-Christian loved ones and friends redemptively, we must be clear on the parameters of orthodox faith. We must have prayer coverage from other Christians with whom we are in community. We must be patient in criticism and enduringly loving. In a word, we must be continually transformed by God's grace in close enough proximity to our family members that they will be touched and drawn to Christ through our lifestyle witness initially.

Fumiko (Housewife): Miracle Turnaround

I first heard the gospel when a friend shared it with me. There was a crisis in my life, and in the midst of the stress, my friend's lifestyle witness and testimony (along with a pastor's Bible message given in our home) made me think I wanted to become a Christian.

About four years after I was baptized, my 29-year-old son was killed in a tragic accident. He was a believer, so even in the midst of my pain, I took great comfort in knowing he was in heaven with Jesus. About a year later, my husband was told that he had terminal cancer and would not live long. My pastor prayed for him and miraculously my husband was healed so completely that he was able to go back to work!

I became passionate about telling others about Jesus because of the hope and comfort I had received concerning my son and my husband. Two of the people I subsequently led to Christ have led others to Christ. I have found it very helpful to develop a trust relationship with people I am working with in order to witness Christ to them effectively.

❦

Fumiko did not immediately start sharing Christ once she believed. It took a dramatic loss and miraculous healing to spur her to begin sharing the comfort and hope she received from God with those around her. Fumiko attends a traditional church, and makes it a habit to intentionally use church events to form redemptive friendships.

These friendships have resulted in the development of several new disciples who have gone on to make other disciples. Fumiko is a fruitful "in-house" disciple multiplier.

19

HOW MULTIPLIERS ARE MADE:
RELATIONAL ENVIRONMENTS

The reason we need revival is because we have forsaken our love relationship with God. God invites us to repent and return to Him. His word to the church at Ephesus indicates that failure to repent is fatal. When He said He would remove their lampstand, He was referring to the church (Rev 1:20). To the extent that we fail to return to our first love, we will miss out on the abundant life God intends, and a lost world will continue its march into a hopeless eternity (Blackaby, Blackaby, & King, 2009)[27]

1) Start where people are
2) Read what they need
3) Know where to take them
    (Comer, 2013)[28]

Relational small groups transform participants and expand the reign of Jesus Christ through disciple multiplication in any context–Christendom, Post-Christian, Persecution.

---

[27] Henry & Richard Blackaby, Claude King. (2009) *Fresh Encounter: God's Pattern for Spiritual Awakening.* p. 58.

[28] Gary Comer. 2013. *Soul Whisperer: Why the Church Must Change the Way It Views Evangelism.* p. 3.

Scripture tells us that as believers we should have "rivers of living water flowing from our innermost being" (John 7:8 NIV). However, most of us find that we are not much different than those we see around us. We might feel like the parched dry reservoirs in California that I see when I'm out on my bike! Where is the life-giving water? Going deeper with God in a relational small group is the best answer to get the living water flowing once again or more consistently in each of our lives.

There are many excellent resources that can help us to lead small groups that will produce disciple multipliers.[29] What they all have in common is they lead to relational communities with transparency, heart transformation, and missional engagement.

Missional "disciple maker culture" does not happen without heart change in a relational context. Three factors are key to leading to the kind of transformation that multiplies disciples:

1) Missionally-focused training that is relationally customized for the Holy Spirit to work in individual disciples. Such training includes vision casting, practice of lessons, and prayerful goal setting for accountability

2) Inductive teaching, incorporating reflection and peer instruction, that results in discovery learning by the disciple that leads to intrinsic motivation for application

3) Interactive prayer that enables a disciple to know on a heart level that he or she is the beloved of Jesus, and to lay aside unclean compulsions or other impediments to righteous thinking and action that results in disciple multiplication.

---

[29] Steve Smith & Ying Kai. (2011) *T4T: A Discipleship ReRevolution.* p. 89-283; Neil Cole. (2010) *TruthQuest Facilitator's Guide*
http://www.cmaresources.org/truthquest
Jeff Reed (2003) *Teaching the First Principles*
http://bild.org/resources/first_principles

Relational small groups that incorporate all three transformational factors evidence 4 W's in their operation: **Welcome, Worship, Word,** and **Work**.

Welcome = Small groups have a life cycle. In the early phase, there is a good chance that people do not know one another well.
If non-Christians have been invited, this is even more so.

Make sure that everyone is welcomed immediately when they arrive. Put them at ease and be sure to have light refreshments available. Prepare good discussion and conversation topics to get people talking. For example, you can read the daily paper for ideas on current topics that are not too threatening. Most folks are honestly interested in the warmth of a *genuine community*. Newcomers will initially be suspicious of a "hidden agenda."

Worship = Music and singing can certainly be a part of worship. But for people to worship deeply, it is important to have a certain element of spontaneity. This is exactly what happens when the Holy Spirit is evident. In *Experiencing God,* Henry Blackaby writes, "Revival is when the Holy Spirit has absolute freedom to do what He wants in the Church." [30]

In our own ministry, we have enjoyed worshipful times going around a circle (or just randomly) alliterating the names or descriptions of God: A = Almighty, Awesome, or Absolute Truth, etc.; B = Beautiful, Blood shed for me, etc.; C = Christ, Compassionate God, etc. The idea is to introduce newcomers to worship in a thoughtful, meaningful way and to usher veterans into worship creatively so their guard is down and God can surprise them with His grace.

Newcomers will not know how to worship. When singing, it's helpful to use a well-known song such as *Amazing Grace.* When praying, it can be helpful to simply spend a little time giving heartfelt thanks for our many blessings from the Creator of all.

Word = While this is commonly called Bible, it can be very simple. "Jesus seems to tell us to 'love one another' more than anything else. Why do you think

---

[30] Henry & Richard Blackaby, and Claude King. (2008) *Experiencing God: Knowing and Doing the Will of God.*

this is? What are some practical ways we can do this at home? At work? In our neighborhood? While recreating?"

In pantheistic or post-Christian cultures, we want to avoid turning the meeting into a "let's impress each other with our insights into the scriptures," especially if there are newcomers who might not yet know Jesus, or the Bible. Nothing else will more quickly make them feel like outsiders–and they will never return.

This is a great time to employ discussion questions that stimulate reflection, with opportunities for anyone who wants to can share what they have discovered–and any answer ventured is acceptable. There is intrinsic motivation to apply what we have discovered for ourselves–we "own it" (cf. Appendix I: Church Based Theological Education (CBTE)).

Another great way to keep on track in Bible study is to use SOS questions:

1) **S** = What does the passage say?
2) **O** = What is this passage calling me to obey?
3) **S** = Who can I share this with? Lord, show me who you
   want me to share this truth with.

One real good study is the "one another" passages of scripture. Ask the SOS questions about such passages.

Work = There are two components to this segment of the meeting. First, we equip ourselves to represent Christ effectively in our own individual contexts. Second, we seek ways to serve together.

Equipping:

1. List your friends and acquaintances you meet regularly who need Christ in their lives. In listing them, include how you commonly contact them, how often, their interests, and prayer needs you are aware of—then PRAY together for those listed on each other's lists. Ask God who you should include on your list, and for hints of how to pray for each person specifically.

2. Pray for one another to boldly but gently "gossip" Christ in your homes, workplaces, and neighborhoods.

3. Pray for one other, bearing one another's burdens--especially when a member shares a struggle or difficulty. For encouragement directly from the Lord that often results in heart change, look for the link to RPM prayer (Appendix I).

Serving:

Ask God to reveal to you the needs around you that he wants you to address in His name. If we are consecrated to do his will, he will make his will clearly known. Christ is the Builder of his Church, we are just his workers. He wants us to declare His excellencies through deed as well as word.

In one cell group we were a part of, one member had cerebral palsy and had never been accepted in his life—even by his own family. It was truly transformational for the men in the cell to come alongside Yoshi and make him feel like a valued part of the group. His life became radiant as a result of cell life and he became a vibrant witness for Christ to family and friends.

Choose a ministry service project together once a month or whatever frequency works for your group. There are many, many opportunities to reach out to poor, disabled, and marginalized people in your area. This kind of service transforms you and your group as much—if not more--as those you will serve.

20

HOW MULTIPLIERS ARE MADE:
EXPONENTIAL CHURCH SYSTEMS

Peter Gelb, General Manager of the Metropolitan Opera of New York, is reinventing opera at the Met.

A few years ago, he saw that the Met clientele was shrinking and aging. Something had to be done. He decided to re-tool the Met in order to make opera as popular with young people as it was a hundred years ago.

First, the operas were adapted to utilize images that were more familiar to people today. Next, the new Met was streamed to viewers through a variety of media, to make Met operas accessible to people who otherwise would not have the opportunity to experience this new approach to opera.

Now crowds of younger people are thrilled by operas that utilize modern images, spectacular sets, and special effects. The "opera message" is once again popular and thriving.

This is the kind of retooling we need if the Church is to thrive and create a culture of disciple multiplication for this generation. Simply implementing a new program or changing the worship music is not enough—and heaven knows, these small changes have sometimes split churches! The goal of ministry leadership is to develop mature, obedient disciples (Matt 28:18-20; Eph 4:13) who live faithfully and fruitfully for their King. These disciples will draw others attracted by the new life in Christ they see evidenced by these transformed men and women of faith.

Beginning with the end in mind, let's consider the process needed to achieve our objective. It's time to let go of even our cherished programs if they do not move us toward transformation and fruitfulness in Christ. New and unfamiliar territory will need to be explored and embraced. We now become acutely aware of our need for *real community*--community that supports us in this quest, community where we can be restored when we fall.

To begin, lets look at the charge Christ gave his Church when he ascended to heaven (Matthew 28:18-20; Mark 16:15-18; Luke 24:46-49; John 20:21-23; Acts 1:7-8). Simply put, the Church exists to provide a venue for ordinary people to encounter Jesus Christ, be transformed by the encounter, and woo others to the feast of grace.

The Disciple Maker Discipleship Flowchart (Figure 10) illustrates a sequence, or series of processes, that together create a culture of genuine multiplication in a church. Disciples that are reached through relational outreach are higher in quality and, in time, quantity. This flowchart model—as any model—of necessity simplifies reality.

I am indebted to the authors of the book *DiscipleShift*.[31] The five discipleship shifts the authors present were a great help in teaching the class Disciple Multiplication and Church Growth at Sabah Theological Seminary in Malaysia in 2013. It was our main textbook and during class discussion we developed the flow chart found in Figure 10. The five necessary church culture shifts Putnam, Harrington, and Coleman identify are as follows:

- From reaching people to making disciples
- From informing to equipping disciples
- From program to purpose
- From activity to relationship
- From accumulating to deploying

Making these shifts require some major paradigm shifts in how church is done and what objectives we should be seeking to fulfill.

I will present some discussion questions after the flow chart in Figure 10 to help us flesh out what these shifts could look like and how we can get there in our specific context.

---

[31] Jim Putnam, Bobby Harrington with Robert Coleman. (2013) *DiscipleShift: Five Steps that Help Your Church to Make Disciples Who Make Disciples.*

21

DEVELOPING A CHURCH CULTURE OF MULTIPLICATION

Developing a church culture of multiplication involves specific processes for every spiritual level, and systems to handle the dynamism of real life disciples:

1. **Infants** need a disciplined, systematic discovery of truth in community. Consider using a truth discovery system such as *TruthQuest*, or *Church Based Theological Education* (**www. BILD.org/**). These and other resources utilize individual reflection and peer teaching in community as integral components that result in discovery learning. What the learner discovers for him or herself carries within it the built-in motivation to apply what he or she has learned in their life. This helps to develop empowered believers who are also equipped to take an active role as redemptive agents in the general culture. In a multiplication culture, disciples are developed to help them reach their full potential in Christ.

2. **Children** need to focus on heart change (from Self-centered to Christ-centered). This involves ongoing discovery learning of the Word, transparent relationships, and transformational interactive prayer that releases to Jesus the self-protective tendencies that hinder the gracious inner working of the Holy Spirit in our lives. This type of interactive prayer also affirms the pray-er and gradually transforms the one who seeks God. Such transformational interactive prayer is administered in close community where personal vulnerability before God can be experienced in a setting of non-threatening assurance of confidentiality and acceptance.

While the three examples of interactive prayer I've featured in this book in *Better Than Acceptable Recovery,* vary a little in their approaches, all three have the goal of taking someone to Christ for affirmation, healing, or release of some kind. They can all be helpful in your development of a culture of multiplication. Christ is still the only one who can set the captive free, bind up the broken-hearted, and restore sight to the blind. No amount of information can heal such deep problems that hinder individual spiritual growth, and divide or pollute the community.

3. **Youth** need to shift their focus from service for Christ to intimate devotion to Christ. This can happen through mentoring or coaching in the skills and attitudes vital for God-honoring service that multiplies. Young believers can learn as they "present their bodies as living sacrifices," and serve alongside Christ experiencing him more deeply in the midst of that service. In Titus 2:6 NKJV, young men are exhorted to be sober-minded. This is the intentionality of the more mature adult in Christ. The shift from duty to devotion also comes as God affirms the spiritual youth in interactive prayer and helps him or her come to a transformational conviction of their new and eternal identity in Christ. Interactive prayer in trusted community is where the morphing spiritual youth can hear affirmation from their loving Heavenly Father directly. Continuing discovery Bible study is a lifelong process—ever deeper and farther in. And close fellowship with more mature believers who can provide vital mentoring and coaching is vital in this relational maturing process.

4. Spiritual **Parents** now serve from a heart of devotion. They are intentional in seeking God first and serving him second.

They know that this direct connection with their Head is the foundation from which all good and lasting things flow. As a result of their close walk with Jesus, they bear much fruit, abiding consistently (if imperfectly) in Christ. Their hearts are continually refreshed by the love and acceptance of their Papa. Others who encounter these spiritual parents want to follow along as they are drawn by the Spirit they sense in them. The Holy Spirit directs willing Spiritual Parents to mentor or coach younger believers where there is a mutual interest. The process begins anew as Spiritual Infants begin the process of transformation in Christ that is the core of what it means to be a disciple. The Spiritual Parent committed to finishing his or her race well will take the attitude of a lifelong learner, will have one or two trusted mentors or coaches who know them well, and will receive affirmation, challenge, and repeated times of spiritual renewal directly from their loving Heavenly Father.

Figure 10. Disciple Maker Discipleship Flowchart

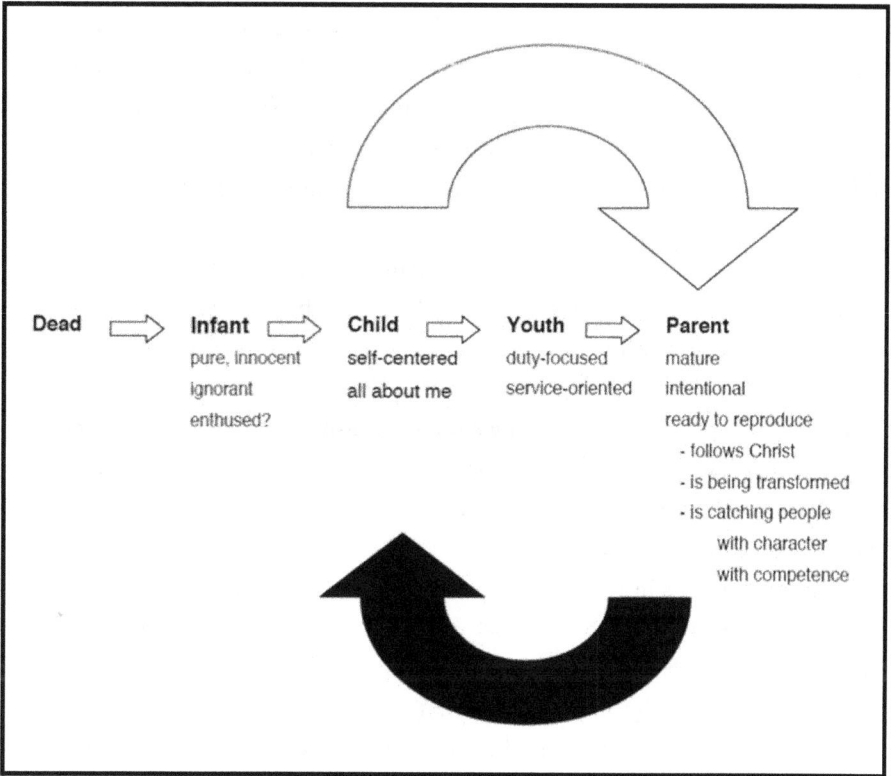

Looking at the flow chart, one might surmise that a believer progresses linearly from **Death/Unsaved** (Ephesians 2:1-2) to **Infancy/New Believer** (1 Corinthians 3:1-3; Ephesians 2:4-7), **Spiritual Child** (Romans 12:10; Philippians 2:1-4; 2 Cor. 12:20-21; Galatians 5:16-21), **Adolescent Youth/ Young Man or Young Woman** (Matthew 16:23; Acts 10:9-29; Ephesians 4:1-3; Titus 2:1-10; Hebrews 10:24-25; James 5:16; 1 Peter 5:5), and finally **Mature Believer/Mature Disciple/Spiritual Parent** (2 Corinthians 3:17-18; Galatians 5:13; Colossians 3:16; 1 John 4:12).

However, a person could be service-oriented in the church (Youthful Adolescence), while simultaneously a selfish child at home (Spiritual Child), and at the same time a fruitful evangelist in the workplace (Reproducing Parent). In reality, every believer is a unique mixture of maturity and immaturity, with strengths and weaknesses co-existing simultaneously in different areas. Therefore, it is essential that our churches have structures in place to catch people when they fall and restore them to the place of connection with the Father and continuing growth in Him.

The large arrows in Figure 10 indicate the dynamic and multi-level nature of most believers (upper white arrow), and the tendency we can have to swing back and forth from self-centeredness (Spiritual Child) to devotion to Christ, and then back again (lower black arrow). This dead-end pendulum is a ticket to mental, emotional, and spiritual meltdown. Notice the back tracking black arrow *always* leads to the self-centered spiritual child. Only ongoing personal heart change through an intimate, growing relationship with God that includes a community component can free us from this self-defeating cycle.

There was a time when I was a mature adult minister in my role as an evangelist for a Tokyo church. But at home, I had a pretty short fuse and would sometimes blow up like a petulant child. When called to serve my family beyond the norm, I sometimes did so out of an adolescent sense of duty rather than joy. I was a "mature" minister, but was too often living like a spiritual adolescent or even child.

The Lord has had to work on me to bring me to greater maturity in all realms of life: my family, my neighbors, the Church, and the Lord. It has been painful—but these growing times with the Lord have become deeper and sweeter. And they have resulted in a deeper, more consistent maturity in my personal life and in my walk with the Lord. I must admit though that Papa is not done with teaching me to walk hand in hand with him in every circumstance.

Christ wants to bring each of us into alignment with our true inherited identity and maturity (Ephesians 4:13). This means all of us—from the first time church attender to the veteran pastor—need ongoing transformation by our Savior. Multiplier discipleship is a lifetime journey.

22

DISCIPLE MAKER CHURCH SYSTEMS DEVELOPMENT QUESTIONS

To help us make the shifts and fill in the gaps necessary to create a culture of disciple multiplication in our churches, I've developed the following discussion questions for church leadership teams.

1. **Unsaved people**

a) How can we reach out to those without spiritual ears? How can I be a friendly messenger of hope, acceptance and love without preaching?

b) How can we help unbelievers develop spiritual ears?

c) How can we compellingly get the gospel to those who have ears to hear?

d) How can we motivate and equip our members to start with where their unsaved friend is; read what their friend needs; take them where their friend needs to go?

2. **Infants**

a) How can we ground them in the Word so that it is more than just head knowledge?

b) How can we encourage their enthusiasm and support their witness?

c) How can we encourage and equip them to continue to grow in all four areas mandated in the Word?

d) How can we hold them accountable, and evaluate their progress without discouraging them?

e) How can we keep their love for Christ strong and growing?

Michael L. Wilson

3. Children

a) How can their affections shift to Christ?

b) How can their heart change? (live more sacrificially exhibiting the fruit of the Spirit more consistently)

c) How can they learn to die daily to self and live for Christ?

d) How can they love God more?

e) How can their affections be captured by Jesus?

4. Youth

a) How can they love God more?

b) How can they grow in devotion to Christ?

c) How can they become "a friend of God?" "Christ's fellow worker?"

d) How can they be restored when they slip into self-centered childishness?

e) How can they have genuine joy in serving? How will we know?

5. Parents

a) How can they walk step by step with the Holy Spirit? (Gal. 5)

b) How can they be mindful of Christ moment by moment? (John 15)

c) How can they help other believers grow to maturity?

d) How can they be restored when they are tempted and slip into self-centered childishness?

A Final Word...

Now in my 60s, I can say without a doubt that growing as a disciple of Christ has its ups and downs. I am so glad for Christ's promise that we will someday know him like he knows us—he knows our very DNA. Just imagine knowing Almighty God that way (1Corinthians 13:12)!

In this "three steps forward, two steps back" process of growing in the grace of God, consecrating oneself is a key concept (John 7:17; Joshua 3:5; 7:13). Our usefulness to God is not so much dependent on how holy we are, but how committed we are to growing in holiness with his help. Anyone who in humble devotion wills to do his will receives grace.

I was one for whom Christ left the other 99 to find. I am so grateful for Christ's persistence in pursuing me.

Appendix I: Releasing Prayer Ministry and other Ministry Links

The links are all found at (copy and paste into your browser if interested): http://whereintheworldismike.com/2014/08/09/exponential-culture-believer-transformation-disciple-multiplication/

1. *Releasing Prayer Ministry* (RPM4). Prayer in triads that results in closer intimacy with Christ and needed heart change in disciples.

2. *Parable of the Talents* (animated video, powerfully biblical, but without words)

3. *Parable of the Sower* (animated video, powerfully biblical, but without words)

4. *Church Based Theological Education: Teaching the First Principles* (small group curriculum for empowered, equipped disciples)

5. *TruthQuest* (theological discovery system used worldwide to develop empowered, fruitful disciples)

7. *Changing Educational Paradigms* (an entertaining video that shows the need for a paradigm shift in teaching methods)

Appendix II: Pre-evangelism Adventure

SPIRITUAL TREASURE HUNTING

(A STORY OF A PRE-EVANGELISM EXPERIENCE

BY MY DAUGHTER AND HER FRIEND J.)

I met up with my friend J the other day at Ikebukuro station in Tokyo with plans to do a treasure hunt. J just graduated from her first year at the HRock School of Supernatural Ministry, and we both have a heart for Japan so we were very excited about this opportunity to try treasure hunting in Tokyo. I say "try," because we really weren't sure how it would go.

This special kind of treasure hunting came out of Bethel Church in Redding, California and involves first asking God for specific clues, and then going out and looking for who the clues point to and offering to pray for them because they are God's treasure! The idea is for ministry to be a joyful game with our Papa God, rather than a chore or an agenda to get people to church. The clues may be locations, physical traits, apparel, objects, names--pretty much anything that could be used to lead us to a specific person. As we listen to God and jot down a list of clues, what's great is that we can't mess it up. There are countless stories of people doing treasure hunts who thought they were just making up a clue but then it turned out to be freakishly accurate and/or God did something amazing. Even if we didn't get any clues about someone, if we feel like we want to approach them we should go for it, cause we're all God's treasures anyway, right? =) It all comes down to enjoying Holy Spirit's presence as we bless precious people and share God's love for them--what fun!

So J. and I ate takoyaki (fried, breaded octopus ball) in a small food court in Ikebukuro station (NW Tokyo) and scribbled out our lists of clues. We mostly got objects, apparel, and a couple location clues.

Then we set out into the gray train station hallways flowing with masses
of people in a hurry to get somewhere. We wandered through the crowds
overwhelmed. Soon we realized we needed a better plan for how to approach
people. J could speak some Japanese, but not enough to explain that we were on
a treasure hunt or to pray for people, thus I was responsible for communication,
whether speaking for myself or translating for J. This meant what we could
say was limited to my vocabulary and ability to communicate--which I don't
even have confidence of in English. How would Japanese people react to being
approached by a stranger telling them they are God's treasure and asking to pray
for them? With all the cults in Japan, I knew Japanese people were often very
nervous about strange religious people and practices. None the less, we decided
to just explain things as best we could.

"We're on a treasure hunt, but it's a special kind of treasure hunt. We asked God
for clues and got [this] and [this] and see, you match that, so we believe you're
God's treasure. Would you mind if we pray a prayer of blessing for you?" -- was
basically the awkward, fumbling script we decided on. I was terribly nervous
because I couldn't imagine a Japanese person responding well to that. However,
we decided that as long as we honored Holy Spirit and stepped out in faith and
love, we couldn't fail.

It was so scary for me! We wandered around for a long time and finally
J. suggested we start with a location I had gotten as a clue: Starbucks. At
Starbucks we ordered drinks and headed up the stairs to the second and
third floors. It was so packed we had trouble finding a seat! We scanned the
room looking for clues. One of J's clues had been a dog with floppy ears,
and she noticed a baby holding a toy dog made of plastic with floppy cloth
ears. "I think she's my treasure, but you'll need to do the talking." J said. I
cringed. The room was filled with 20 or so Japanese people sitting around
studying, reading, chatting, using their computers, but it was so quiet and
the woman with the baby was sitting right in the middle of the room. "I
don't think I can do it." I said, looking out the window at the rainy sky and
gray buildings.

"That's ok, no pressure," said J. I sighed.

I sat there for a long time, struggling internally and making excuses externally, but finally I finished my drink and looked over at the woman and her baby with determination. They were God's treasure. Holy Spirit wanted to bless her--it was time to have some faith and get over myself. Ha!

So we went over and J> said "Hi" and I started to translate, when the woman asked us if we'd prefer English. I was shocked. So Josie stepped up and explained the treasure hunt to her and blessed her and her baby and had a nice little conversation. I was so relieved not to have all the pressure on me, and my fear started to dissipate. We knew it was a God thing!

After that we returned to the station and had a number of other encounters. One of my clues had been orange wedge high heels, and we actually found a woman with those exact shoes. She was Chinese but spoke great Japanese and we had a nice little talk with her and were able to pray for her.

The last encounter was one of my favorites though, because J had gotten "chocolate" or "a chocolate shop" and we'd been looking but hadn't been able to find one, even by checking the directory. Then we wandered into a different area and all of a sudden there it was. A shop devoted to chocolate! There were three women working in the little shop, but I had also gotten black-rimmed glasses and I felt like we were supposed to pray for the woman who wore those glasses. When we approached her and explained about the treasure hunt and how she fit the clues she got so excited. Just hearing how she had been chosen specifically by God was so overwhelming to her. We told her how much God loves her and how precious she is to him and that we had come to bless her (I don't know if this made sense to her but she was still very happy). J. prophesied over her and I translated and it was just so awesome!!

Even with our often clumsy attempts to bless people and share God's love with them, I believe Holy Spirit was with us and honored in our interactions.

Though I had been worried about the reactions we would get from our strange explanation of what we were doing, everyone we approached actually greeted us warmly and I felt like they saw us as real people, rather than as potential creeps or religious fanatics, so I was really thankful for that. lol

I want to add that, though I think doing ministry is great, I believe it's also really important not to stop there, but that it truly become a way of life rather than simply an event we go out and do. If we're not comfortable blessing the people around us in our daily lives, how authentic is our outreach? Do we put on an act during times of intentional ministry or is it really who we are? Let's not forget to pursue the greater, all-encompassing lifestyle of the Kingdom.

God is good!! =)

Appendix III: Profile of an Evangelistic Multiplier— "Closers" — 10 Qualities to be on the lookout for in "movement starters"

Listed by strength of correlation in the research participants (strongest to weakest)
Strongest →

1. His superiors perceive him as in the know technically even though he has less technical expertise than innovators or inventors.
2. She is well respected by her peers.
3. People often seek his advice.
4. She is seen as a primary resource person by those around her.
5. He is an excellent role model.
6. She is socially active—she has a wide circle of friends and acquaintances.
7. He is a leader whether or not he holds a formal leadership position.
8. She is more innovative than the average individual.
9. He is able to withstand criticism and rejection with grace.
10. She is comfortable with attention—more than the average person.
→ Weakest

References
(Rogers, 2004), (Rogers, 2003), (Wilson, 2009b)

Appendix IV: Detox from Strictly Cognitive Bible Study

Lectio Divina: Detox from Years of Strictly Cognitive Bible Study for Jesus' sheep who have trouble hearing the still, small whisper of God.

Lectio Divina ("Holy Reading"): This is a link to directions on how to engage in Bible study that engages more than just the head. It is a great way to connect with God in Bible study and grow attuned to his gentle whispers. Thanks, monks of Saint Andrews Abbey in Valyermo, Calif. This is one of the places we enjoy a prayer retreat once or twice a year (more when we can).
http://www.saintandrewsabbey.com/SearchResults.asp?Cat=35

Lectio Divina does not end the need for rigorous Bible study. It is an excellent complement to it.

'Love the Lord your God with all your *heart* and with all your *soul* and with all your *mind* and with all your *strength*.'

The second is this: 'Love your neighbor as yourself.' (Mark 12:30-31).

Bibliography

Allen, R. 1962. *The spontaneous expansion of the church and the causes which hinder it* ([1st American ed.). Grand Rapids,: W.B. Eerdmans Pub. Co.

Arthur, K. 1994. *God, are you there?* Eugene, Or.: Harvest House Publishers.

Barna, G. 1990. *The frog in the kettle : what Christians need to know about life in the year 2000.* Ventura, Calif., U.S.A.: Regal Books.

Barna, G. 2009. *The seven faith tribes : who they are, what they believe, and why they matter.* Carol Stream, Ill.: BarnaBooks/Tyndale House Publishers.

Barna, G. 2011. *Maximum Faith: Live Like Jesus: Experience Genuine Transformation.* Jointly: Ventura, CA; New York, New York; Glendora, CA: Jointly: Metaformation Inc., Strategenius Group LLC, WHC Publishing.

Barna, G. 2013. Next GEN Pack: Barma Group.

Blackaby, H. T., Blackaby, R., & King, C. V. 2009. *Fresh encounter : God's pattern for spiritual awakening* (Rev. & expanded ed.). Nashville, Tenn.: B&H Group.

Blackaby, H. T., & King, C. V. 2008. *Experiencing God : knowing and doing the will of God* (Rev. & expanded. ed.). Nashville, Tenn.: Broadman & Holman Publishers.

Boren, M. S. 2010. *Missional small groups : becoming a community that makes a difference in the world.* Grand Rapids, Mich.: Baker Books.

Bugbee, B. 2005. *Discover your spiritual gifts the network way : 4 assessments for determining your spiritual gifts.* Grand Rapids, Mich.: Zondervan : Willow Grace Resources.

Cheney, J. M. S. E., ThD. 1999. *Jesus Christ: The Greatest Life.* Eugene, OR: Paradise Publishing, Inc.

Clinton, D. J. R. 1999. Clinton Biblical Leadership Commentary CD: Clinton Resources **http://www.bobbyclinton.com/**.

Cole, N. 2005. *Organic church : growing faith where life happens* (1st ed.). San Francisco: Jossey-Bass.

Cole, N. 2010 revision. *TruthQuest: The Search for Spiritual Understanding*. Signal Hill, CA: CMAResources.

Coleman, R. E., & Fish, R. J. 1986. *The master plan of evangelism*. Old Tappan, N.J.: F.H. Revell.

Comer, G. S. 2013. *Soul Whisperer: Why the Church Must Change the Way It Views Evangelism*. Eugene, OR: Resource Publications an imprint of Wipf & Stock Publishers.

Eymann, D. 2012. Turnaround Church Ministry: Causes of Decline and Changes Needed for Turnaround. *Great Commission Research Journal*, 3(2): 146-160.

Farrar, S. 1995. *Finishing strong : how a man can go the distance*. Sisters, Or.: Multnomah Books.

Fee, G. D., & Stuart, D. K. 2002. *How to read the Bible book by book : a guided tour*. Grand Rapids, Mich.: Zondervan.

Fee, G. D., & Stuart, D. K. 2014. *How to read the bible for all its worth* (Fourth edition. ed.). Grand Rapids, MI: Zondervan.

Frost, M. 2006. *Exiles : living missionally in a post-Christian culture*. Peabody, Mass.: Hendrickson Publishers.

Frost, M., & Hirsch, A. 2003. *The shaping of things to come : innovation and mission for the 21st-century church*. Peabody, Mass.: Hendrickson Publishers.

Fujino, G. 2006. Ukiyoe Church Planting: Layers and Evangelism in Japan. *Japan Harvest*, 58(2): 12-15.

Gladwell, M. 2002. *The tipping point : how little things can make a big difference* (1st Back Bay pbk. ed.). Boston: Back Bay Books ; Little, Brown.

Goldmann, R. 2006. Are We Accelerating or Inhibiting Movements to Christ? *Mission Frontiers*, 28:5(Sept-Oct 2006): 7.

Greer, S. *Freedom, Healing and Deliverance, A Practical Guide for Setting Others Free*.

Gumbel, N. The ALPHA Course. London, UK.

Gupta, P. R., & Lingenfelter, S. G. 2006. *Breaking tradition to accomplish vision : training leaders for a church-planting movement : a case from India*. Winona Lake, Ind.: BMH Books.

Hawkins, G. L. a. P., Cally. 2008a. REVEAL: Follow Me: What's Next for You?: 160. Barrington, IL: The Willow Creek Association.

Hawkins, G. L. a. P., Cally. 2008b. REVEAL: Where Are You? Barrington, IL: The Willow Creek Association.

Hawkins, G. L. a. P., Cally. 2009. REVEAL: Focus: The Top Ten Things People Want and Need from You and Your Church: 120. Barrington, IL: The Willow Creek Association.

Huizing, R. L. 2012. In Search of the Healthy Church: A Meta-Ethnographic Study. *Great Commission Research Journal*, 4(1): 43-59.

Hull, B. 2006. *The complete book of discipleship : on being and making followers of Christ*. Colorado Springs, CO: NavPress.

Hybels, B. 2010. *The power of a whisper : hearing God, having the guts to respond*. Grand Rapids, Mich.: Zondervan.

Jenkins, P. 2007. *The next christendom : the coming of global Christianity* (Rev. and expanded ed.). Oxford ; New York: Oxford University Press.

Jensen, R. A. 1993. *Thinking in story : preaching in a post-literate age*. Lima, Ohio: C.S.S. Pub.

Kimball, D. 2007. *They like Jesus but not the church : insights from emerging generations*. Grand Rapids, Mich.: Zondervan.

Knowles, M. S., Holton, E. F., & Swanson, R. A. 2011. *The adult learner : the definitive classic in adult education and human resource development* (7th ed.). Amsterdam ; Boston: Elsevier.

Krause, W. S., William James Putnam, Avery T. Willis Jr., and Brandon Guindon. 2010. *Equipping Disciples who Make Disciples: Real-Life Discipleship Training Manual*. Colorado Spring, CO: NavPress.

Kreider, A. 1999. *The change of conversion and the origin of Christendom*. Harrisburg, Pa.: Trinity Press International.

Kylstra, C., & Kylstra, B. 2005. *Biblical healing and deliverance : a guide to experiencing freedom from sins of the past, destruction beliefs, emotional and spiritual pain curses and oppression*. Grand Rapids, Mich.: Chosen.

Kylstra, C. a. B. 2007. *Restoring the Foundations: An Integrated Approach to Healing Ministry* (2nd Edition ed.). Hendersonville, NC, USA: Proclaiming His Word Publications.

Laubach, F. C. 1964. *Frank Laubach's prayer diary*. Westwood, N.J.: Revell.

Lewis, R. L., & Lewis, G. 1983. *Inductive preaching : helping people listen*. Westchester, Ill.: Crossway Books.

Logan, R. E. Story that changed his discipleship, *https://loganleadership.com/*.

Logan, R. E. 2013. Seven Discipleship Models: Logan Leadership.

Logan, R. E., Carlton, S., & Miller, T. 2003. *Coaching 101 : discover the power of coaching*. St. Charles, IL: ChurchSmart Resourses.

MacNutt, F. 1995. *Deliverance from Evil Spirits: A Practical Manual*. Grand Rapids, MI: Chosen Books, a division of Baker Books.

Max7. Parable of the Sower.

Max7. Parable of the Talents.

Mayers, M. K. 1987. *Christianity confronts culture : a strategy for crosscultural evangelism* (Rev. and enl. ed.). Grand Rapids, Mich.: Academie Books.

McIntosh, G. L. 2012. The Impact of Church Age and Size on Turnaround. *Great Commission Research Journal*, 4(1): 6-14.

Miller, D. E., & Yamamori, T. 2007. *Global Pentecostalism : the new face of Christian social engagement*. Berkeley: University of California Press.

Minatrea, M. 2004. *Shaped by God's heart : the passion and practices of missional churches* (1st ed.). San Francisco, CA: Jossey-Bass.

Miyake, R. a. o. 2013. Releasing Prayer Ministry: 27.

Murphy, E. 2003. *The Handbook for Spiritual Warfare, Revised and Updated*. Nashville, TN: Thomas Nelson Publishers, Inc.

Neighbour, R. W., Jr. 1991a. *Part 1: Building Bridges, Opening Hearts*. Singapore: Touch Outreach Ministries

P.O. Box 19888

Houston, TX 77224, USA

or

Touch Resources
#06-00/07-00
66/68 East Coast Road
Singapore 1542.

Neighbour, R. W., Jr. 1991b. *Part 2: Building Groups, Opening Hearts.*
    Singapore: Touch Outreach Ministries
P.O. Box 19888
Houston, TX 77224, USA
or
Touch Resources
#06-00/07-00
66/68 East Coast Road
Singapore 1542.

Neighbour, R. W., Jr. 1992. *Part 3: Building Awareness, Opening Hearts.*
    Singapore: Touch Outreach Ministries
P.O. Box 19888
Houston, TX 77224, USA
or
Touch Resources
#06-00/07-00
66/68 East Coast Road
Singapore 1542.

Nouwen, H. 2011. The Lord's Beloved.

O'Connor, J. P., & Patterson, G. 2006. *Reproducible pastoral training :
    church planting guidelines from the teachings of George Patterson.*
    Pasadena, Calif.: William Carey Library.

Penfold, G. 2012. Characteristics of Turnaround Pastors. *Great Commission
    Research Journal,* 3(2): 177-196.

Peterson, E. H., & Thomas Nelson Publishers. 2007. *The message-NKJV
    parallel Bible.* Nashville, TN: Thomas Nelson.

Precept Ministries International. *The new inductive study Bible (ESV).*

Priddy, K. E. 2012. Church Turnaround: Perspectives, Principles, and Practices.
    Great Commission Research Journal, 3(2): 161-176.

Putman, J., Harrington, B., & Coleman, R. E. 2013. *DiscipleShift : five steps that help your church to make disciples who make disciples*.

Rath, T. 2007. *Strengths finder 2.0*. New York: Gallup Press.

Reed, J. 2003. *Teaching the First Principles: First Principles of Leading the First Principles*. Ames, Iowa: LearnCorp Resources, BILD International.

Riesen, R. A. 2010. *The Academic Imperative: A Reassessment of Christian Education's Priorities*. Colorado Springs, CO: Purposeful Designs Publications.

Rogers, E. M. 2003. *Diffusion of Innovations* (5th edition ed.). New York: The Free Press: A Division of Simon and Schuster, Inc.

Rogers, E. M. 2004. A Prospective and Retrospective Look at the Diffusion Model. *Journal of Health Communications*(9): 13-19.

Rosenberg, J. C. 2009. *Inside the revolution*. Carol Stream, Ill.: Tyndale House Publishers, Inc.

RSAnimate. Changing Educational Paradigms.

Rumsley, D. D. 2012. Sideways Leadership: Perceptions of the Senior Pastor's Transformational Leadership Style and Its Relationship to Church Effectiveness. *Great Commission Research Journal*, 4(1): 15-33.

Ryken, L., & Ryken, P. G. 2007. *The literary study Bible : ESV : English Standard version, containing the Old and New Testaments* (ESV text ed.). Wheaton, Ill.: Crossway Bibles.

Sandford, J., & Sandford, P. 1982. *The transformation of the inner man*. South Plainfield, NJ: Bridge Pub.

Scazzero, P., & Bird, W. 2010. *The emotionally healthy church : a strategy for discipleship that actually changes lives* (Updated and expanded ed.). Grand Rapids, Mich.: Zondervan.

Scazzero, P., & Scazzero, P. 2010. *The emotionally healthy church workbook : 8 studies for groups or individuals* (Updated and expanded ed.). Grand Rapids, Mich.: Zondervan.

Smith, E. M. 1999. *Beyond Tolerable Recovery: Moving beyond controlled behavior, strong determination, self-effort, and just "getting better" into genuine life-changing, maintenance-free victory*. Campbellsville, KY: Family Care Publishing.

Smith, S. w. Y. K. 2011. *T4T A Discipleship ReRevolution*. PO Box 1884 Monument, CO 80132: WIGTake Resources

Steffen, T. 2011. *The Facilitator Era: Beyond Pioneer Church Multiplication*. Eugene, OR: Wipf and Stock.

Toyotome, M. D. 1968. *Enjoyable Personal Evangelism*. Manila, Philippines: Christian Literature Crusade.

Vella, J. K. 2002. *Learning to listen, learning to teach : the power of dialogue in educating adults* (Rev. ed.). San Francisco, CA: Jossey-Bass.

Vella, J. K. 2008. *On teaching and learning : putting the principles and practices of dialogue education into action* (1st ed.). San Francisco: Jossey-Bass.

Von Kamel, D. R. 2012. Closing Our Doors: Ten Reasons to Consider Why Your Church May Be in Trouble…and What to Do. *Great Commission Research Journal*, 4(1): 34-42.

Vun, W. 2009. *Who Is Building Whose Church?* Kota Kinabalu, Malaysia: Kingdom Harvest Ministries P.O. Box 21872, 88776 Luyang, Kota Kinabalu, Sabah, Malaysia.

Webster, J. 2001. *The Voice: Hearing God's Voice with Clarity, Consistency, & Confidence*. Lanham, MD: Pneuma Life Publishing.

Wilkes, A. P. 1944. *The Dynamic of Service*. Kansas City, MO: Beacon Hill Press.

Wilkinson, B. 1999. *The three chairs : experiencing spiritual breakthroughs*. Nashville, Tenn.: LifeWay Press.

Wilkinson, B. 2006. *30 Days to Experiencing Spiritual Breakthroughs*.

Wilson, J. C. 1994. *More to be desired than gold : a collection of true stories* (2nd ed.). South Hamilton, MA: Gordon-Conwell Theological Seminary.

Wilson, M. 2010. Teaching for Transformation. In A. McMahan (Ed.), *Great Commission Research Journal*, Vol. 2: 110. La Mirada, CA: Cook School of Intercultural Studies.

Wilson, M. L. 2009a. Evangelism at the Family Altar. In Cook School of
      Intercultural Studies., & Great Commission Research Network. (Eds.),
      Great Commission Research Journal, Vol. 3. La Mirada, CA: Cook
      School of Intercultural Studies.

Wilson, M. L. 2009b. ***Japanese Christian Multiplication: A
      Phenomenonological Study***. Biola University, La Mirada, CA.

Young, S. 2004. ***Jesus calling : enjoying peace in His presence : devotions for
      every day of the year***. Nashville: Integrity Publishers.

Young, S., Young, S., & Young, S. 2011. ***Jesus calling devotional Bible : New
      King James Version***. Nashville: Thomas Nelson.

ABOUT THE AUTHOR

Michael was born in Los Angeles, California into a family where alcohol and the family dynamic that accompanies it was all too common. He accepted Christ as his Savior at camp when 12. For two years he hungrily read the scriptures and prayed for transformation of himself and his family. When 14 years old, he became discouraged and gave up and turned from God. He tried life in the wilderness for 13 years and found that no amount of material success could satisfy the thirst in his heart.

After a series of serious accidents, Michael surrendered to his Lord Jesus once more and began life anew with Christ. He had no plan to work in Asia but God led him first to China for a summer and then Japan for much longer. His marriage to Mary Jo has been a great blessing in his life and huge confirmation that Jesus loves him more than he can imagine.

While working with Japanese churches to develop new churches, he earned a doctorate in Church Multiplication through Biola University. Michael has extensive experience multiplying disciples and has taught disciple multiplication and church growth on a number of continents. Plans are in place for this volume to be published in other languages through God's amazing networking!